World

Through The

Eyes Of Scriptures

By
Dr. Sahadeva dasa

B.com., FCA., AICWA., PhD
Chartered Accountant

Soul Science University Press

www.DrDasa.com

Readers interested in the subject matter of this
book are invited to correspond with the publisher at:
SoulScienceUniversity@gmail.com   +91 98490 95990
or visit DrDasa.com

First Edition: January 2014

Soul Science University Press expresses its gratitude to the
Bhaktivedanta Book Trust International (BBT), for the use of quotes by
His Divine Grace A.C.Bhaktivedanta Swami Prabhupada.

ISBN 97893-82947-05-9

Published by:
Dr. Sahadeva dasa for Soul Science University Press

Printed by:
Rainbow Print Pack, Hyderabad

To order a copy write to chandra@rgbooks.co.in
or buy online: Amazon.com, Rgbooks.co.in

Dedicated to....

His Divine Grace A.C.Bhaktivedanta Swami Prabhupada

Ordinary men see through their eyes, Cows see by smell, kings by spies and the learned through the scriptural knowledge.
~ Mahabharata

By The Same Author

Oil-Final Countdown To A Global Crisis And Its Solutions

End of Modern Civilization And Alternative Future

To Kill Cow Means To End Human Civilization

Cow And Humanity - Made For Each Other

Cows Are Cool - Love 'Em!

Let's Be Friends - A Curious, Calm Cow

Wondrous Glories of Vraja

We Feel Just Like You Do

Tsunami Of Diseases Headed Our Way - Know Your Food Before Time Runs Out

Cow Killing And Beef Export - The Master Plan To Turn India Into A Desert
By 2050

Capitalism Communism And Cowism - A New Economics For The 21st Century

Noble Cow - Munching Grass, Looking Curious And Just Hanging Around

Spare Us Some Carcasses - An Appeal From The Vultures

To Save Time Is To Lengthen Life

Life Is Nothing But Time - Time Is Life, Life Is Time

An Inch of Time Can Not Be Bought With A Mile of Gold

Lost Time Is Never Found Again

Cow Dung - A Down-To- Earth Solution To Global Warming And Climate
Change

Cow Dung For Food Security And Survival of Human Race

(More information on availability on DrDasa.com)

Contents

The Author

Preface

Different people perceive the world differently. No two perceptions are ever the same. We think of the world as we are. In fact the world is different than the way we see it.

Most of our paradigms are inaccurate because we do not have all of the information. We think we do but we don't. When we receive additional or new information it often causes us to rethink and change our paradigm.

Stephen Covey, the famous author tells the story of being on a subway one Sunday morning when a man and his children board a train. Immediately the kids start running up and down the train car annoying riders, yelling, screaming and knocking papers out of people's hands.

Finally Covey could no longer stand the apparent disregard and discipline this parent was showing. He addressed the man, "Mister, you need to correct your children, they are bothering the passengers."

The man looks up from his daze and takes notice, "Oh, I'm sorry. We just left the hospital where their mother died about one hour ago. I guess they don't know how to handle it and frankly I don't either."

Covey says his paradigm immediately shifted from being critical to being empathic. The new information changed the way he saw the situation, caused different behavior and got a different result.

Challenge your assumptions about yourself, others, situations, and things. The world transforms as you transform yourself. The key to personal effectiveness is to change our paradigms, our assumptions, the way we see the world.

A young couple moved into the house next to a church compound. A few days later, the pastor's wife called the pastor into the kitchen. She was peering out the window. "Look at our neighbor hanging the wash out on the line. That laundry is still dirty! She must be a newlywed who doesn't know how to wash clothes properly. Maybe she's not using enough laundry soap."

The pastor urged his wife not to say anything, but the next week, sure enough, the neighbor's dirty laundry hung on the line again. And again the following week. Every time the pastor's wife peered out the window, she saw her neighbor's dirty laundry hanging on the clothesline.

Then, one morning as she scurried around getting breakfast, the pastor's wife exclaimed, "Look! She finally got the clothes clean! I wonder who helped her?"

The pastor smiled and said, "Honey, no one helped her. I just got up early this morning and cleaned our windows!"

Similarly we need to rinse our mind and intellect in the light of transcendental knowledge. In Vedic terminology this is known as 'cheto darpana marjanam', cleansing the mirror of heart and mind.

Srila Prabhupada explains, "A person who acts exactly according to the tenets of scripture is called *sastra-caksus*. *Sastra-caksus* means one who sees through the eyes of the authorized scriptures. Actually, any man of knowledge and experience should see everything through these books. For example, with our naked eye we perceive the sun globe simply as some glaring substance, but when we see through authorized books of science and other literature, we can understand how much greater the sun globe is than this earth and how powerful it is. So seeing things through the naked eye is not actually seeing. Seeing things through the authorized books or authorized teachers is the correct way to see."

Sahadeva dasa

Dr. Sahadeva dasa
1st January 2014
Secunderabad, India

1

Fixing The Earth Up - A Story

We were told good planets are hard to find, dont blow it but we did it anyways. Now our leaders want to fix up the Earth in big big summits. This is like the proverbial village fella who fixed the moon up long ago.

Story goes like this. A villager went to get water from the well at night. When he looked down in the well, he saw the moon's reflection in the water. Thinking that the moon had fallen from the sky, he ran to get a rope with a big hook on it. He pitched it into the well so hard that the hook snagged on a rock.

The fellow gave a huge tug and the hook came free, flying up and out of the well. It knocked him right over. As he fell, he noticed the moon in the sky. Standing up, he said, "It's true that I strained and struggled, but thank God, I got the moon back in its place."

Similarly, our world leaders are trying to tug the Earth out of the well of despoilment. Earth is God's property and living here in accordance with God's ways or natural ways wouldn't create all

this mess. But our leaders think that they are controllers of nature and they can blow it or set it right whenever they want. It is all theirs and it is under their absolute control.

This foolish arrogance is costing us dearly. Now the latest attempt to "tug the moon out" is being made at Copenhagen in December 2009. Leaders of over a hundred nations have confirmed their participation. Known as 'Climate Summit', this gathering has been organized by United Nations.

The leaders would try to cut the carbon emission and save the planet, of course without creating a fundamental change in the life style and consciousness. But that would only mean, 'resolutions, dissolutions, revolutions... and no solutions'. We are not alone in thinking like this. James Hansen, a leading NASA scientist who helped alert the world to dangers of global warming, told the Guardian newspaper that the planet would be better off if the forthcoming Copenhagen climate change talks ended in collapse. As per him, any agreement likely to emerge from the negotiations would be so deeply flawed that it would be better for future generations if we were to start again from scratch. Hansen is strongly opposed to carbon market schemes, in which permits to pollute are bought and sold, seen by the European Union and other governments as the most efficient way to cut emissions and move to a new clean energy economy.

Hansen adds, "I would rather it not happen if people accept that as being the right track because it's a disaster track, Tackling climate change does not allow room for the compromises that govern the world of politics. This is analogous to the issue of slavery faced by Abraham Lincoln or the issue of Nazism faced by Winston Churchill. On those kind of issues you cannot compromise. You can't say let's reduce slavery, let's find a compromise and reduce it 50 percent or reduce it 40 percent."

Therefore solution lies in making a fundamental shift in the way we think or creating a change of consciousness or heart or as suggested by Hansen, 'starting from scratch'. All our actions flow from our consciousness or the way we think, feel and will. As told by Einstein, "no problem can be solved from the same level of consciousness that created it."

Rampant materialism lies at the root of our environmental crisis. The solution lies at turning our face towards spiritual development, once again.

Its heartening to see that several influential environmental organizations in the world, though secular by constitution, are echoing this theme.

One such forum is Worldwatch Institute, an independent research organization that works for an environmentally sustainable and socially just society, in which the needs of all people are met without threatening health of the natural environment or well-being of future generations.

Alan Durning of Worldwatch Institute writes, "In a fragile biosphere, the ultimate fate of humanity may depend on whether we can cultivate a deeper sense of self-restraint, founded on a widespread ethic of limiting consumption and finding non-material enrichment...Those who seek to rise to this environmental challenge may find encouragement in the body of human wisdom passed down from antiquity. To seek out sufficiency is to follow the path of voluntary simplicity preached by all the sages from Buddha to Mohammed. Typical of these pronouncements is this passage from the Bible: "What shall it profit a man if he shall gain the whole world and lose his own soul?"

Allen adds,"....action is needed to restrain the excesses of advertising, to curb the shopping culture, and to revitalize household and community economies as human-scale alternatives to the high consumption lifestyle. There could be many more people ready to begin saying "enough"....After all, much of what we consume is wasted or unwanted in the first place. How much of the packaging that wraps products we consume each year - 162 pounds per capita in the United States - would we rather not see? ...How many of the unsolicited sales pitches each American receives each day in the mail - 37 percent of all mail - are nothing but bothersome junk? How much of the advertising in our morning newspaper - covering 65 percent of the newsprint in American paper - would we not gladly see left out?"

Allen continues, "How many of the miles we drive - almost 6,000 a year a piece in the United States - would we not happily give up if livable neighborhoods were closer to work, a variety of local merchants closer to home, streets safe to walk and bicycle, and public transit easier and faster?

Keith C. Heidorn sums this up when he defines 'Living Gently' as a voluntary manner of living which pursues a positive, satisfying life that is considerate, noble and easily managed and that seeks to produce as small an impact on the environment as possible. It is a lifestyle chosen not only for personal satisfaction, but also for the good of our fellow inhabitants of planet Earth: animals, humans and plants. It involves frugality but goes beyond.

Overall Spiritualization of Society - Bad Theology Creates Bad Ecology

Humanity is on a "spiral to suicide" and that the environmental discourses of academia often suggest an 'end-of-the-pipeline approach'. Mary Evelyn Tucker echoes this misgiving. "We're all concerned about simply rhetorical statements or a superficial approach [that] is not going to tap into the deep spiritual reservoirs of people. A spiritual change of heart could only offer a solution towards this 'much talked about and little done for' crisis.

Consumption vs. Self-realization

If the world is ever to become free from the threat of environmental annihilation, we shall have to undertake a thorough reexamination of the materialistic assumptions underlying not only our picture of nature but our conception of our very selves.

Some scientists are already beginning to question whether materialistic principles are really adequate to explain basic features of human existence-such as consciousness. For example, John C. Eccles, a Nobel-prize-winning neurobiologist, states, "The ultimate problem relates to the origin of the self, how each of us as a self-conscious being comes to exist as a unique self associated with a brain. This is the mystery of personal existence." Eccles said that "the uniqueness each of us experiences can be sufficiently explained only by recourse to some supernatural origin."

Thomas Berry mentions that we must reestablish a spiritual "intimacy" with the earth as compared to our overly scientific-technological relationship with the earth. That is only possible when we understand that we are essentially spirit souls and not bodies.

If the conscious self is factually supernatural in origin, and if this knowledge were firmly integrated into our educational and cultural institutions, society would probably be much more directed toward self-realization than it is today. The overwhelming impetus toward the domination and exploitation of matter that underlies today's industrial civilization and culminates in resource crunch would certainly be lessened.

In words of Grandon Harris: Our honeymoon with the planet earth is over. We must take our marriage with the earth seriously. We cannot divorce it, but it can divorce us!

This seriousness, as opposed to frivolousness, comes from understanding our real identity as spirit souls and not as Darwinian monkeys. From a monkey, hardly any seriousness can be expected.

Following verses from Bhagavad-gita illustrate these points.

kamopabhoga-parama, etavad iti niscitah

They believe that to gratify the senses is the prime necessity of human civilization. (Bg 16.11) This verse of Bhagavad-gita tells us that those who mistake their identities or those who fail to understand who they are, they tread the path of sense aggrandizement. Environmental crisis is an outcome of this viewpoint.

Another verse (Bg 2.62) sums up the our consumeristic civilization:

dhyayato visayan pumsah
sangas tesupajayate
sangat sanjayate kamah
kamat krodho 'bhijayate

While contemplating the objects of the senses, a person develops attachment for them, and from such attachment lust develops, and from lust anger arises.

This verse of Bhagavad-gita tells us that by contemplating the objects of the senses one becomes attached to them and ultimately ends up frustrated and bewildered. Industrialized society in particular has as its cornerstone the need to stimulate consumption, to constantly fuel economic growth. To this end, it constantly encourages us to meditate on the objects of our senses. With individuals' desires massively outstripping their abilities to meet their aspirations, it is hardly any surprise that we create ongoing frustration and extreme egotism, which result in environmental, social, and cultural devastation.

Text 4.22, *'yadrccha-labha-santusto'* describes that by practicing bhakti-yoga, one is satisfied with gain which comes of its own accord and one attains a taste for simple living and high thinking. In other words, developing love for God automatically moderates one's appetite for material things by enriching one's life spiritually.

This God consciousness is found aplenty in Srila Prabhupada's books. (BBT.info) Give it a shot and see for yourself.

2.

From Ram-rajya to Rum-rajya

The other day while passing through a shopping area, I witnessed a chaotic scene, a kind of riot. Curious, I got off to have a look. The gold rush was for a bottle of wine. People were pushing, pulling and yelling at each other. Scene could have easily turned violent and it was a volatile situation. I took out my camera and aimed. Several faced turned and some proceeded in my direction. I took a quick shot and retreated, saving myself from a possibly unpleasant experience.

It appeared to me that India was finally catching up. Dreams of leaders like Nehru to see a 'cultured' India was finally coming true.

Back home I sat reflecting for some time, bit saddened by the turn of events for India.

It is apparent that more and more Indians are resorting to alcohol these days. Thanks to the destruction of traditional values, easy spending power and wide availability of brands to choose from, a modernized India is saying cheers.

Around 15 to 20 per cent of Indians consume alcohol and over the past twenty years, the number of drinkers has increased considerably. According to a survey by The Hindustan Times, an estimated 5 per cent of Indians can be classified as alcoholics which means at least fifty million people in India are addicted to alcohol.

Misuse of alcohol has been implicated in over 20 per cent of traumatic brain injuries and 60 per cent of all injuries reporting to emergency rooms. Excessive usage of alcohol has also resulted in deliberate self-harm, high-risk licentious behaviour, HIV infection, tuberculosis, oesophageal cancer, liver disease, duodenal ulcer and many more.

Prior to British rule, bhang, and afeem were major intoxicants in India but their consumption was extremely low. Use of alcohol was limited to Rajas and the upper echelon of society. British rulers opened liquor shops. It became fashionable among Indian Babus to use and offer alcohol at their western style parties. The use of alcohol started among educated and middle class.

Gandhi was opposed to alcohol consumption and on his insistence, the constitution of India incorporated a directive principle of State policy stating that "the State shall endeavour to bring about prohibition of the consumption of intoxicating drinks". In 1977, India imposed total prohibition that lasted two years. But despite all this, alcohol has become "the in thing", a sign of social sophistication and a symbol of prestige. Just a century ago it was condemned and regarded as something alien to local culture.

Srila Prabhupada explains this phenomena: "This gambling, drinking, meat-eating, these things were all unknown in India. They did not know how to drink. These Britishers introduced. There is still a lane, a street in Calcutta, Porterly Street. There was a woman

of suspicious character. She was supplied big bottles of wine, and she used to canvass rich men's son to take wine, and it was distributed free. In this way wine was distributed, and people began to drink gradually. And I have seen a tea committee. They were advertising tea, "You take this tea, you'll not feel hungry, you'll be cured from malaria...," and so many things. And people came and took tea in this way. Now everybody is taking tea. In the morning they'll gather at the tea stall. You see. So people, they did not know what is gambling, what is drinking, what is meat-eating. So these things were introduced gradually." (Lecture on Srimad-Bhagavatam 5.5.2 - London, September 17, 1969)

In another place, Srila Prabhupada explains the reasons behind British eagerness to modify Indian behaviour and thought pattern. "The Britishers were for two hundred years and they preached. Their policy was to kill the Indian culture. Lord McCauley, after studying Indian situation, reported to the Parliament that "If you keep Indians as Indians, you will not be able to rule over them," So therefore there was regular policy to kill Indian civilization. And because they had the governing power, they could do it. Therefore India lost its own culture and was victimized by the Western culture. This is the position. They are learning how to eat meat, how to drink wine, how to dress with coat and pant, how to go to the hotel, illicit sex. (Morning Walk - Durban, October 13, 1975)

Due to its large population, India has been identified as the potentially third largest market for alcoholic beverages in the world. This has attracted the attention of multi-national liquor companies. Sale of alcohol has been growing steadily at 6% and is estimated to grow at the rate of 8% per year.

Srila Prabhupada adds, "There is a story that one man was drinking. So, drinking in India is a great sin. So his friend advised that "You are drinking. You'll go to hell." So he said, "Oh, my father also drinks." So he said, "Your father also will go to hell." "Oh, my brother also drinks." "Oh, he also will go to hell." In this way, he continued to say, "My father, my brother, my sister, my this, my that..." And he was replying, "Yes, he will also go to hell." Then the drunkard replied, "Oh, hell is heaven. Because we're all drinking here and we will drink there. So what is that hell? That is heaven." (Lecture, Los Angeles, June 27, 1972)

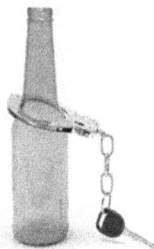

Barely three decades ago, less than 1% of the cases in psychiatric wards were admitted for alcohol-related problems; now the number exceeds 30% in most of the major psychiatric centres.

Nothing has worked to contain this growing menace of drinking. Legislative measures like prohibition, awareness programs by social organizations, educational propaganda by social activists, nothing has had any success so far. Only solution is to get the drunkards and everyone else hooked up to a much stronger liquor, a liquor far more stimulating than Vodka, bourbon, brandy, gin or rum. It goes by the brand name of *'namasava'*, or booze of Holy Name. This brand is owned by the liquor baron Sri Nityananda. He Himself is an addict and has a global marketing network. Free sample of this prestigious label is shipped to any one who calls out the following mantra:

hare krishna hare krishna krishna krishna hare hare
hare rama hare rama rama rama hare hare

Thakura Bhaktivinode, the Marketing Director for Sri Nityananda Inc. says:

anudina jeno, tava nama gai,
kramete krpaya tava
aparadha ja'be, name ruci ha'be,
aswadibo namasava

If I sing Your name every day, then gradually by Your mercy the ten offenses will disappear, taste for Your holy name will grow within me, and then I shall relish the intoxicating wine of that name. *(Saranagati)*

3.

What Do Cannibals Look Like?

Take A Look In The Mirror

Human taste buds have grown tired of all the flesh and blood we gorge upon daily. To the tickling taste buds, what could be more savory than a cute little baby, killed in the womb itself.

Sounds abhorring? Read on. Senomyx is an American biotechnology company working toward developing additives to amplify certain flavors and smells in foods. The company claims to have essentially "reverse engineered" the receptors in humans that react for taste and aroma, and that they are capitalizing on these discoveries to produce chemicals that make food taste better. Senomyx develops patented flavor enhancers by using "proprietary taste receptor-based assay systems." These receptors have been previously expressed in HEK293 cells.

HEK stands for human embryonic kidney cells. These cells, originally come from a "healthy, electively aborted human fetus." Using information from the human genome sequence, Senomyx has identified hundreds of taste receptors and currently owns 113 patents on their discoveries. Senomyx collaborates with seven of

the world's largest food companies to further their research and to fund development of their technology. Ajinomoto Co., Kraft Foods, Cadbury Adams, PepsiCo, Firmenich SA, Nestlé SA, and Solae all collaborate with Senomyx, but do not specify where its additives may be found in their products.

Senomyx's products work by amplifying the intensity of flavors. Because very small amounts of the additive are used, Senomyx's chemical compounds will not appear on labels, but will fall under the broad category of "artificial flavors." For the same reason, the company's chemicals have not undergone the FDA's usual safety approval process for food additives. Senomyx's MSG-enhancer gained the Generally Recognized as Safe (GRAS) status from the Flavor and Extract Manufacturers Association, an industry-funded organization, in less than 18 months, which included three months of tests on rats.

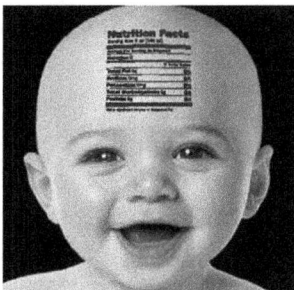

According to Senomyx's website, it "received a positive review by the Joint FAO/WHO Expert Committee on Food Additives, which determined that there were no safety concerns with the use of the Company's savory flavor ingredients in foods. The positive assessment by JECFA is expected to expedite regulatory approvals in a number of countries, particularly those that do not have independent regulatory approval systems."

Senomyx's revenues for the last quarter of 2007 were up 87% from the same period in 2006, and its stock prices are rising. CEO Kent Snyder reports that corporate goals include "continuing to achieve significant progress in all of our discovery and development programs such as regulatory approval for our S2383 sucralose enhancer and selection of a sucrose enhancer for regulatory development. We also expect expanded commercialization of food products containing our savory flavor ingredients and additional new business development accomplishments."

US Agency Rules Pepsi's Use Of Aborted Fetal Cells In Soft Drinks Constitutes 'Ordinary Business Operations'

Saturday, March 17, 2012 by: Ethan A. Huff, staff writer

The Obama Administration has given its blessing to PepsiCo to continue utilizing the services of a company that produces flavor chemicals for the beverage giant using aborted human fetal tissue. LifeSiteNews.com reports that the Security and Exchange Commission (SEC) has decided that PepsiCo's arrangement with San Diego, Cal.-based Senomyx, which produces flavor enhancing chemicals for Pepsi using human embryonic kidney tissue, simply constitutes "ordinary business operations."

The issue began in 2011 when the non-profit group Children of God for Life (CGL) first broke the news about Pepsi's alliance with Senomyx, which led to massive outcry and a worldwide boycott of Pepsi products. At that time, it was revealed that Pepsi had many other options at its disposal to produce flavor chemicals, which is what its competitors do, but had instead chosen to continue using aborted fetal cells -- or as Senomyx deceptively puts it, "isolated human taste receptors."

A few months later, Pepsi' shareholders filed a resolution petitioning the company to "adopt a corporate policy that recognizes human rights and employs ethical standards which do not involve using the remains of aborted human beings in both private and collaborative research and development agreements." But the Obama Administration shut down this 36-page proposal, deciding instead that Pepsi's used of aborted babies to flavor its beverage products is just business as usual, and not a significant concern.

"We're not talking about what kind of pencils PepsiCo wants to use -- we are talking about exploiting the remains of an aborted child for profit," said Debi Vinnedge, Executive Director of CGL, concerning the SEC decision. "Using human embryonic kidney (HEK-293) to produce flavor enhancers for their beverages is a far cry from routine operations!"

Back in January, Oklahoma Senator Ralph Shortey proposed legislation to ban the production of aborted fetal cell-derived flavor chemicals in his home state. If passed, S.B. 1418 would also reportedly ban the sale of any products that contain flavor chemicals derived from human fetal tissue, which includes Pepsi products as well as products produced by Kraft and Nestle.

Sources for this article include:

http://en.wikipedia.org/wiki/Senomyx

http://www.lifesitenews.com

http://www.naturalnews.com

Rice With Human Genes

Despite repeated scandals involving the contamination of rice seed stocks with GM variants, the US government has given approval for the large-scale planting of GM rice strains containing human genes.

Having apparently abandoned plans to use their GM rice as an additive to animal feedstuffs, Ventria Bioscience is initially aiming to market their human protein-producing rice as a cure for diarrhoea in developing countries. Since diarrhoea can be highly effectively and inexpensively treated with simple rehydration salts, producing a GM alternative is clearly an absurdity.

This has led to speculation that sick children in developing countries are being used in a cynical campaign of pretence suggesting that Ventria Bioscience is motivated by altruism. Their longer-term plans are to include the GM human proteins in yoghurt, granola bars and sport re-hydration drinks.

Do we really need a GM cure for diarrhoea? Is it acceptable to release GM rice into the environment where it will inevitably contaminate other rice strains? Do we really find it acceptable to consume human proteins? Even Ventria's own scientific publications have raised questions about safety.

Background

The United States Department of Agriculture (USDA) has recently taken the first steps towards allowing the large-scale cultivation of three varieties of genetically manipulated (GM) rice containing human genes.[1] These rice strains, created by the California-based company Ventria Bioscience, have been genetically engineered to carry the human genes encoding lactoferrin, lysozyme, or serum albumin. After a public comment period, which ended on 30 March 2007, a decision was taken to allow these GM strains to be cultivated on 3,200 acres of land in Kansas, USA.

Almost simultaneously with this announcement, the USDA revealed the discovery that rice seed stocks in Arkansas had become contaminated with a different GM strain, LL62, which had never been approved for commercial production. This embarrassing discovery was made during an investigation into the widespread contamination of US rice by yet another GM strain, LL601, raising serious concerns about the safety measures in place to contain GM crops.

Rice With A Human Touch?

Each GM strain created by Ventria Bioscience contains a human gene encoding one of three proteins: lactoferrin, lysozyme, or serum albumin. Lactoferrin and lysozyme are antimicrobial proteins found, in human breast milk, and in tears and saliva. Serum albumin is one of the protein constituents of human blood.

But What's It For?

Initially, Ventria Bioscience tested its GM lactoferrin and lysozyme as a possible addition to animal feedstuffs, as an alternative to antibiotics.[2] The widespread use of antibiotics in animal feedstuffs is well documented to have led to the emergence of antibiotic-resistant microorganisms, potentially endangering human health.[3,4]

Having apparently abandoned plans to market the GM rice for animal feedstuffs, Ventria have now tested it on children in Peru as a possible treatment for paediatric diarrhoea.[5] Elsewhere, they have talked about plans to include it in yoghurt, sports drinks, and granola bars.[6]

Do We Really Need A GM Treatment For Diarrhea?

Although diarrhoea causes more than 2 million deaths per year, mostly in developing countries, its causes are well understood and its treatment simple and reliable. Most cases of diarrhoea last only a day or two, and the patient fully recovers without any treatment at all. Only in more prolonged cases is treatment required to prevent the patient becoming from dehydrated. In such cases, the administration of simple oral rehydration salts is highly effective.

The GM human proteins were tested on Peruvian children as an addition to oral rehydration therapy. One third of the patients received conventional oral rehydration salts, one third received a rice-based oral rehydration salts, and the others received the rice-based therapy with the addition of the GM human proteins.[5]

Ventria did not claim that this led to a higher recovery rate, since all the children recovered, but that the addition of the GM proteins increased the speed with which the patients recovered. Simply put, the children treated with the oral rehydration salts plus the GM human proteins recovered in about 4 days, rather than about 5 days.[5] Hardly the miracle cure that Ventria would like us to believe.

Since diarrhoea can be very effectively treated with simple and inexpensive oral rehydration salts, which are easily transported and can be stored without refrigeration, do developing countries really need to buy a more expensive, genetically manipulated alternative from Ventria Biosciences? Clearly not.

But Is It Safe?

Following the trial in Peru, questions have been raised whether the parents of the children were adequately informed that the experimental treatment involved GM human proteins. This has led to an inquiry in Peru.[7] Safety issues were also raised when the parents of some of the children in the trial claimed that their children had subsequently suffered moderate to severe allergic reactions.[8]

The GM proteins have biological activity in human beings, but have never been tested as a drug and have never received FDA approval for use as a drug. So nobody can claim with complete certainty that they pose no danger to human health.

What About Containment?

Since there are clearly safety questions concerning the consumption of these GM human proteins, how can we be sure when we buy a bag of rice that it has not been contaminated with a GM strain? We can't. As mentioned above, there are already well documented – and very recent – examples of GM rice contaminating rice destined for human consumption. No matter what safety measures are put in place, mistakes will always happen.

Also, when a GM organism is released into the environment, it is probably going to be out there, in some form or other, forever. Cross pollination can transfer GM traits into regular strains. Do we have the right to take such decisions on behalf of future generations?

And Another Ethical Issue...

The recent contamination scandals in the USA have indicated that it is very likely that Ventria's GM rice would eventually find its way onto our plates, if their plans were allowed to proceed. Even aside from any safety issues, we all have to ask ourselves if we find it acceptable to eat human proteins in any form at all. If Ventria were to go ahead with plans to include their GM human proteins in yoghurt, would we really find it ethically acceptable to eat that yoghurt? In countries such as India, where a significant proportion of the population is vegetarian, is it ethically acceptable to introduce an 'animal' protein into one of the staples of their diet, let alone a human protein?

Conclusion

Any one of the issues raised would be sufficient to convince almost anybody that permission should not be granted for the large-scale planting of Ventria's GM rice. But taken together, the environmental, health and safety, and ethical issues, surely add up to an overpowering argument that the plans of Ventria Bioscience to cultivate GM rice containing human genes must be stopped.

By DebraBroughton, Friends of the Earth International

References:

1.Department of Agriculture, Animal and Plant Health Inspection Services. Ventria Bioscience; Availability of an environmental assessment for field tests of rice genetically engineered to express lactoferrin, lysozyme, or serum albumin. Docket No. APHIS-2007-006, Federal Register Vol. 72, No. 30, Wednesday, February 28, 2007. Available from: http://www.epa.gov/fedrgstr/ EPA-IMPACT/2007?February/Day-28/i3484.htm

2.Humphrey, BD, Huang, N, Klasing, KC. Rice expressing lactoferrin and lysozyme has antibiotic-like properties when fed to chicks. J Nutrition. 2002;132:1214-1218.

3.World Health Organisation. Overcoming antimicrobial resistance: WHO report on infectious diseases (2000) WHO, Geneva, Switzerland.

4.World Health Organisation Fact Sheet No 194, WHO, Geneva, Switzerland.

5.Zavaleta, N, Figueroa, D, Rivera, J, Sanchez, J, Alfaro, S, Lonnerdal, B. Efficacy of rice-based oral rehydration solution containing recombinant human lactoferrin and lysozyme in Peruvian children with acute diarrhea. J Pediatr Gastroenterol. 2007;44:258-264.

6.http://www.aphis.usda.gov/brs/aphisdocs/04_30901r_ea.pdf. See corresponding citation for lactoferrin at http://www.aphis.usda.gov/brs/aphisdocs/04_30201r_ea.pdf

7.Leighton, P. Study on infants in Peru sparks ethics inquiry. Science and Development Network, July 18, 2006.http://www.scidev.net/content/news/eng/study-on-infants-in-peru-sparks-ethics-inquiry.cfm

8.Diaz, D. Transgénicos: Niños ya sufren sus efectos. La Republica, Peru, July 14, 2006.

Srila Prabhupada:

They'll eat everything. This godless civilization will lead people to such condition of life. *Kadharya bhaksana kare, tara janma adho pate yaya.* This life they will eat everything, all nonsense thing, and next life they become pig, cats, dogs. That's all. This will be.

They'll kill their own children and eat. That time is coming. Nature's law is that you grow your own food. But they are not interested in growing food. They are interested in manufacturing bolts and nuts.

The killing process is so nice that it goes up to the point of killing one's children. That is now happening. Killing business has so expanded that they are killing their own children. Just see the influence of Kali-yuga. The children, they take shelter of the father and mother, thinking very safe. Now, in this Kali-yuga, even there is no safety under the care of father and mother. Just see how this material civilization is progressing. Very, very dangerous. *Kalau nasta-drsam.* Therefore that Bhagavata verse is there,

krsne sva-dhamopagate
dharma-jnanadibhih (saha)
kalau nasta-drsam (esa)
puranarko 'dhunoditah

Very, very abominable condition in this age of Kali. Very, very. It is the beginning of Kali. Now we have to pass through 427,000's of years. Kali-yuga will make progress in that way. And people are now practicing eating their children, and at the end of Kali there will be no food available. They'll have to eat the children just like the snakes do.

(Lecture, Sri Caitanya charitamrta, Adi-lila 1.13, Mayapur, April 6, 1975)

4.

The Cucumber Crisis

Lowly cucumber has emerged as a culprit in a national scandal. Our repertoire of crises seems to have no end in sight. Monsanto cucumbers are causing genital baldness and have been banned in Nova Scotia with immediate effect.

Robin Steel reports that a six-month study by AgriSearch, an on-campus research arm of Dalhousie University, has shown that genetically modified (GM) cucumbers grown under license to Monsanto Inc. result in serious side effects including total groin hair loss and chafing in "sensitive areas", leading to the immediate and total ban of sales of all that company's crop and subsequent dill pickles.

Srila Prabhupada explains: "This should be broken, and this should be done." Then another man comes. He breaks the same thing again. Unless there is control over the mind, it will dictate something new: "Do it like this." There was a Bengali poet. He also sung a song, *ek ta nutana kichu koro*: "Do something new." This is mind's business. He is not satisfied with the old things. *Nutana kichu koro.* So that's a very big song. Why change? The whole material world

is like that. *Ei nutana kichu koro*: "Do something new," and be implicated. We are not satisfied with old things.

But the Vedic civilization is that "Do not try to invent some order. That will create disturbance. Be satisfied. Whatever you have got by nature's way, be satisfied. Don't spoil your time. Save your time for Krsna consciousness." That is Vedic civilization. (Lecture on Srimad-Bhagavatam 5.6.4, Vrndavana, November 26, 1976)

The tracking study of 643 men and women in Nova Scotia came about after reports began to surface about bald field mice and the bald feral cats that ate them being discovered by farmers on acreages growing the new crop.

"The bald wild animals raised a huge flag and we immediately obtained subpoenas for the medical records of all 600 plus adults who took part in focus groups and taste tests of the cucumbers by Monsanto in Canada," said Dr. Nancy Walker, Director of Public Health Research at Dalhousie. "Fully 3/4 of the people who ate these cukes had their crotch area hair fall out. This is not a joking matter at all...these people now have hairless heinies."

Nova Scotia became the first province or state in North America to ban a Monsanto GM food product, although GM corn and other food crops are currently outlawed in Ireland, Japan, New Zealand, Germany, Austria, Switzerland, Greece and Hungary. Governments in Australia, Spain, UK, France, Turkey, India and Mexico have public petitions or legislative bills under consideration. Californians recently voted down a bill that would have required all GM foods to be clearly labeled. Monsanto cucumbers have been ordered removed from all food stores in Nova Scotia, while Quebec stores have begun a voluntary removal, partially because the UPC code stickers contain some English.

"I pulled down my boxer shorts to get ready for bed one night and there it was...a pile of hair that looked like a chihuahua puppy," said Eric LaMaze, who was paid $50 by Monsanto to compare the tastes of natural cucumbers to Monsanto GM cucumbers in March of this year in Halifax. "Then I saw my bits and whoa they were like all shiny skin. Bald."

Mr. LaMaze and other taste test participants said the GM cucumbers tasted the same as the naturally grown cucumbers but made a slight "fizzing noise" when swallowed. The participants also complained of raw skin in their genital area and some bed wetting.

Monsanto Inc., a self-described Sustainable Agriculture Company based in Creve Coeur, Missouri, where they share offices with major shareholder Bain Capital, issued a statement saying, "Next generation fruits and vegetables, including VO5 cucumbers, are safe for human consumption with some potential minor side effects. Some fine-tuning is underway."

McDonald's Corp. issued a statement following the Nova Scotia ban announcing that they will replace dill and sweet cucumber pickles on their burgers with non-GM pickled zucchini as a precaution until it is proven that no Monsanto pickles were sold into the North American market.

Federal Minister of Health Leona Aglukkaq said a Canada-wide recall and ban will be issued within 24 hours. "The Government of Canada takes this very, very seriously," said the Minister. "Being hairless down there should be a matter of personal choice for Canadian men and women and not one taken away by a cucumber."

"They used to have the real cucumber slices in those salad things at the City Hall Dining Club," sighed Former Toronto Mayor Rob Ford on the courthouse steps after being impeached by a Provincial Judge. "Those were good times..."

Srila Prabhupada comments: The demons possess wonderful and supernatural powers to create material wonders. But they are always disturbing elements of the society. The modern demons are the harmful material scientists who create some material wonders for disturbance in the society. (Srimad Bhagavatam SB 1.15.8)

5

Modern Civilization

A Pig's Fart?

Fifteen firefighters And Two Trucks Attend To A Pig's Farts

On November 26th 2009, it was the 1st anniversary of terrorist attack on the Mumbai. Whole of India was put on high alert. On the same day, there was another kind of scare on the other side of the globe. A flatulent pig sparked a gas emergency in southern Australia when a farmer mistook its odours for a leaking pipe.

Fifteen firefighters and two trucks rushed to a property at Axedale in central Victoria state after reports of a gas leak. When the firefighters got there, as they drove up the driveway, there was this huge sow, about a 120-odd kilo sow, and it was very obvious where the gas was coming from.

"We could not only smell it, but we heard it", said fire captain Peter Harkins. The pig's owner was "a little bit embarrassed" and it took fire crews a little while to compose themselves.

This is an instance where arrangement is very grand but outcome is nil. In Sanskrit this is known as 'bahvarambhe laghu kriya'. Arambha, beginning is very gorgeous but end is hardly of any significance. A high grade arrangement with zero outcome! Sounds like our modern civilization where every thing is decked up but everything, including our very lives, are completely hollow and empty.

So much technological advancement and progress! Has it made our lives richer in anyway, or happier than our predecessors in any way, other than threatening the very existence of the world?

Like the pig in the story, our civilization is polluting everything, externally the environment and internally the global consciousness.

Is our progress simply a high grade arrangement with zero or negative outcome?

Srila Prabhupada explains the phrase '*bahvarambhe laghu kriya*' in a lecture. (Stockholm in 1973)

"In the material world, everything is *bahvarambhe laghu kriya*. That has been spoken by Canakya Pandita. *Aja yuddhe muni sraddhe. Ajah* means goats. You have seen goat fighting? As if two big heroes are fighting. But as soon as somebody comes: "Hut!" they'll go away. Have you seen, experienced? Goats and lambs, they'll fight: (makes sound:) "Onh, onnh." Like this. But, but as soon as somebody comes: "Hut!" So this is one of the example of *bahvarambhe laghu kriya*.

Arambha, as if something very serious going to happen. But actually it is nonsignificant. *Aja yuddhe muni sraddhe. Muni*, in the jungle, in the forest, there are *munis*, sages. So they are arranging for some festivals to offer oblations to the forefathers, *sraddha*. So what they have got? They have got some fruits and leaves. That's all. So the arrangement may be that "Tomorrow, we are going to have this festival." But the festival means some leaves and some water. That's all. No utensils, no gold, no jewels, nothing of the sort. So this is another *bahvarambhe laghu kriya*. Arrangement is very big, but fact is nothing. And *dampatya kalahe caiva*. And fight between or quarrel between husband and wife. In India, there is no question of divorce. So nobody takes very serious care when there is fight between husband and wife. So there also: "I'm going to immediately leave you, going to kill you…" and so many things. But after an hour, everything is finished. No more quarrel. *Dampatya kalahe caiva prabhate megha-garjane.* And in the morning, if you see big cloud assembly and thundering sound, but you rest assured. There will be no rain in the morning. So these things are *bahvarambhe laghu kriya. Arambha,* beginning is very gorgeous. But end is nothing."

Will our Civilization and all its attendant paraphernalia will prove to be ultimately as trifling and inconsequential as that pig's fart?

Story of 'Much Ado About Nothing'
Himalayan Mountains Give Birth (Parvatan musakodbhavah)

There were big headlines that the Himalayan mountain is going to deliver a child. So people gathered around to see the event. They saw the mountain go into labour and there came one little mouse out of the mountain hole. So they went back satisfied that Himalaya mountain has given birth. One rat!

At least begetting an elephant would have suited the occasion better.

This is our position. Many a times we are devoting life's energies to insignificant things, creating much ado about nothing.

suptasya visayaloko
dhyayato va manorathah
nanatmakatvad viphalas
tatha bhedatma-dhir gunaih
One who is sleeping may see many objects of sense gratification in a dream, but such pleasurable things are merely creations of the mind and are thus ultimately useless. Similarly, the living entity who is asleep to his spiritual identity also sees many sense objects, but these innumerable objects of temporary gratification are creations of the Lord's illusory potency and have no permanent existence. One who meditates upon them, impelled by the senses, uselessly engages his intelligence. (Srimad Bhagavatam 11.10.3)

Whole media is like that Australian pig's fart, colossal hoax, creating issues out of non-issues. Whole so-called terrorism is a byproduct of media frenzy. Because people are glued to their TV sets, terrorists are blasting bombs. If people didn't have time to watch so much television, there wouldn't be so many bomb blasts. All killing is done to show to the world and if the world didn't have time to see all this crap, there wouldn't be so much killing of the innocent. Rise is terrorism is directly related to rise in media exposure of the masses.

Srimad Bhagavatam urges us to hear about the Absolute Truth instead.

srotavyadini rajendra
nrnam santi sahasrasah
apasyatam atma-tattvam
grhesu grha-medhinam

Those persons who are materially engrossed, being blind to the knowledge of ultimate truth, have many subject matters for hearing in human society, O Emperor. (Srimad Bhagavatam 2.1.2)

6.

Moon Landing

Another Humbuggery?

The search for words "Moon Landing Hoax" generates 3.67 million (and counting) hits on Google as on 27th November 2009.

Srila Prabhupada sums up the moon mission thus, "Very gorgeous. The result is sand and rocks. Going to the moon planet, the *arambha* was so much expensive. And the result is to bring some sand and rocks."

At the expense of countless billions and years of research and hard labor, scientists have supposedly gone to the moon. Of course, all they have "brought back" are a few blurry photos, a handful of rocks, and the revelation that the moon is barren. And now they want more money to go to Mars.

What is so marvelous about this? It is complete lunacy. On our own planet earth, millions of people are without food, shelter, and basic amenities. Scientists would be more credible if instead of spending billions of dollars to bring rocks from the moon, they would spend the taxpayer's hard-earned money to improve their own lot on Earth. Rocks are rocks, whether

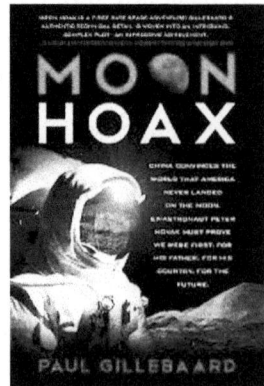

from China, from the moon, or from Mars. Or is it that science can turn the rocks into bread and cheese by applying some chemicals?

Why not be satisfied with whatever planet we have been given to live on. Earth is not so bad after all because living on Earth includes an annual free trip around the Sun.

How Nasa Came To Decide To Land On Moon ;-)

There was this big meeting of scientists and they were unable to decide whether to send the mission to Sun or Moon. Some were in favor of a moon mission while others favored a mission to the Sun. Then one scientist quipped that Sun is too hot for a manned mission. Everyone looked crestfallen as they never thought of this aspect of mission. But then NASA director solved the problem, "We will send the 'astronuts' at night." Hearing this there was smile on everybody's face and they all felt relieved. So the whole mood shifted in favor of going to Sun. But then another senior scientist stood up and spoke thus, "What is more useful: the Sun or the Moon? The Moon, because the Moon shines at night when you want the light, whereas the Sun shines during the day when you don't need it." There was this huge applause and they unanimously decided in favor of going to the Moon.

Of course, after Moon mission, NASA needed more money, so they had to come up with a Mars mission. After few years (and quite a few billion dollars) when the Senate questioned them about Mars mission, they sent the following reply, "It is not conclusive yet, but we at NASA believe that the Mars Pathfinder has found proof of life on Mars. Its CD recorder was stolen."

Look at the following news by AFP.

'Moon rock' Worthless Wood - Says World's Top Museum
Aug 28, 2009

THE HAGUE (AFP) A treasured piece of moon rock showcased in a key Amsterdam museum is nothing but petrified wood, museum authorities said of a gift made to a former Dutch prime minister by the US envoy.

The exhibit at the Rijksmuseum, originally gifted to Willem Drees in 1969 by then US ambassador William Middendorf as a souvenir of a pathbreaking trip by three US astronauts on July 20, 1969.

"When we received it, we insured it for 100,000 florins or 50,000 euros in today's money," said Xandra van Gelder, the editor-in-chief of the museum's internal magazine.

But she told AFP that it was "hardly worth 50 euros," adding that museum authorities had been alerted by space and other experts. This was confirmed by independent studies on the object, which is roughly the size of a matchbox.

The US space agency NASA gifted pieces of the alleged moon rock to several countries.

ya esa sodasa-kalah puruso bhagavan manomayo 'nnamayo 'mrtamayo deva-pitr-manusya-bhuta-pasu-paksi-sarisrpa-virudham pranapy ayana-silatvat sarvamaya iti varnayanti.

Because the moon is full of all potentialities, it represents the influence of the Supreme Personality of Godhead. The moon is the predominating deity of everyone's mind, and therefore the moon-god is called Manomaya. He is also called Annamaya because he gives potency to all herbs and plants, and he is called Amrtamaya because he is the source of life for all living entities. The moon pleases the demigods, pitas, human beings, animals, birds, reptiles, trees, plants and all other living entities. Everyone is satisfied by the presence of the moon. Therefore the moon is also called Sarvamaya [all-pervading].

~ Srimad Bhagavatam 5.22.10

The Rijksmuseum, one of the world's top museums, is better known for its vast collection of paintings by Rembrandt.

Srila Prabhupada, in the Rathayatra parade of San Francisco, 1969, gave his opinion on this Moon thing :

"Perhaps you saw in the San Francisco Chronicle that when I landed at San Francisco airport a reporter asked me my opinion of the landing of your American people on the moon. I asked him whether I should give my frank opinion. He said, "Yes." So I replied that it is "simply a waste of time." If you actually want to transfer yourself from this planet to another planet, then you must follow the principles of the Bhagavad Gita. In the Bhagavad Gita you will find a nice verse which says that there are innumerable planets, not only in this one universe, but there are innumerable universes also. In each of these universes there are millions and trillions of planets, and each planet has a different atmosphere. So even if you go to the moon, you will not be happy there, because everywhere in the material universes the four principles of material conditioning are always present. They are birth, death, old age and disease. But Krishna says that, if one goes back to My Supreme Planet, which is called Goloka Vrindaban, he will never have to come back to this miserable condition of life. This Krishna consciousness movement is to take you to the highest state of eternal bliss and knowledge. It is not a sentimental movement, but is the practical means of perfect spiritual realization. If within this life you practice Krishna

A theologian and an astronomer were talking together one day. The astronomer said that after reading widely in the field of religion, he had concluded that all religion could be summed up in a single phrase. "Do unto others as you would have them do unto you," he said, with a bit of smugness, knowing that his field is so much more complex.

After a brief pause, the theologian replied that after reading widely in the area of astronomy he had concluded that all of it could be summed up in a single phrase also. "Oh, and what is that?" the astronaut inquired. "Twinkle, twinkle, little star; how I wonder what you are!"

consciousness, then you will very easily be able to go to Goloka Vrindaban and have your blissful life, eternal and full of knowledge. You should start this process today. Simply chant *Hare Krishna, Hare Krishna, Krishna Krishna, Hare Hare/ Hare Rama, Hare Rama, Rama Rama, Hare Hare.* I request you to follow this car of Lord Jagannath, and make progress in your life to Goloka Vrindaban, instead of wasting your time for the moon planet."

Exactly After 40 Years - India Wants To Land On Moon

After 40 years of first Moon mission by America, still mired in controversy, India finally wakes up and wants to send a manned mission to the Moon in "next 5 to 10 years". India will do whatever the West does, no matter how nonsensical or absurd.

While millions are underfe and 70% population has no toilet facility and everyday over a hundred farmers commit suicide, India wants to blow billions on a Moon mission, just to catchup with the West. Instead of copying West, India should take a look at its own timeless and immense heritage which can be the guiding beacon for the rest of the world. What is on Moon has already been discovered by the great sages and elaborately mentioned in Vedic literatures.

Srila Prabhupada quoted a saying to explain this point, *"apana dhana vilaya diya bhiksa mange parer dvare* - India, after squandering her own wealth, is begging at others doors" Of course things are improving and India's global image has undergone a change of late.

We can quote here another lecture by Srila Prabhupada given in New York in 1966 to further illustrate this point,

"In a bengali proverb, there is a very nice comparison like this, that *'bara bara ghora gela rasatal, benta ghora bole kata jala'.* That means... You know. The animals, they can swim over the river. So there was a big, overflowing river. So at that time there were no ships, so everyone had to cross river either by small boats or by swimming. Generally the animals were allowed to swim over and men, they took small boats... Now, there was very good current and so many horses were swept away by the current. And one lean and thin horse came. He is asking, "Let me know how much water there is?"

The things that West is becoming fedup with are being eagerly grabbed by India. Blind copying is not good. Copying should be done Intelligently and for one's betterment.

Prabhupada tells an interesting story from colonial India :

"A clerk was making a fair book from the rough book. So he went to the toilet room, and he was jumping into the air and leaping around the room. So all of a sudden his British boss came in.

"What are you doing here?"

"Sir, I am trying to capture one fly."

"And why?"

"I am making the fair copy of the book, but in the original book there is a fly smashed. So I have to paste one fly."

Similar to the story above, Indian media is blindly imitating the western media.

North America has television shows like 'Jerry Springer', 'Jenny Jones', 'Ricki Lake' and 'Montel Williams'. These programs feature guests telling detailed stories of their deviant behaviour, such as mothers sleeping with their daughter's boyfriend, kids who curse and threaten their parents, parents who teach their kids how to shoplift and incest stories at times. It seems as though acceptance or rejection of their deviant behavior is measured by the applause of a degraded audience. Deviancy and immorality are not new in human history. What's new is the willingness of people to put bizarre lifestyles on display to millions of strangers. Even worse is the relative absence of social sanction. Years ago, people would have been personally ashamed if others knew about their corrupt lifestyles. They'd try to hide it rather than go on national television or radio to broadcast it.

Now countries like India are copying these American TV programs. India has an immensely popular version called 'sach ka samana'. Srila Prabhupada called this a 'new crow' phenomenon. Indians are behaving like 'new crows'. When crows eat garbage, after a while they become full. But when a new batch arrives, they are especially eager to taste the garbage.

Why should India copy everything from West. India has unfathomable treasure of Vedic knowledge lying unused in its own backyard.

Astronomy In Ancient India

Ancient India's contribution in the field of astronomy is well known and well documented. Reference to the structure of universe and movement of planets is found in all Vedic literatures. By 500 AD, ancient Indian astronomy emerged as an important part of Indian studies and its affect is also seen in several treatises of that period. In some instances, astronomical principles were borrowed to explain matters pertaining to astrology like casting of a horoscope. Apart from this linkage of astronomy with astrology in ancient India, science of astronomy continued to develop independently, and culminated into original findings, like:

-The calculation of occurrences of eclipses

-Determination of Earth's circumference

-Theorizing about the theory of gravitation

-Determination of number of planets under our solar system

There are astronomical references of chronological significance in the Vedas. Fire altars, with astronomical basis, have been found in the third millennium cities of India. The texts that describe their designs are conservatively dated to the first millennium BC, but their contents appear to be much older.

Yajnavalkya (perhaps 1800 BC) advanced a 95-year cycle to synchronize the motions of the sun and the moon. A text on

Vedic astronomy that has been dated to 1350 BC, was written by Lagadha. In 500 AD, Aryabhata presented a mathematical system to calculated the time it took the earth to spin on its axis and considered the motions of the planets with respect to the sun (in other words it was heliocentric). His book, the Aryabhattiya, presented astronomical and mathematical theories in which the Earth was taken to be spinning on its axis and the periods of the planets were given with respect to the sun.

In this book, the day was reckoned from one sunrise to the next, whereas in his Aryabhata-siddhanta he took the day from one midnight to another.

Aryabhata wrote that 1,582,237,500 rotations of the Earth equal 57,753,336 lunar orbits. This is an extremely accurate ratio of a fundamental astronomical ratio ($1{,}582{,}237{,}500 / 57{,}753{,}336 = 27.3964693572$), and is perhaps the oldest astronomical constant calculated to such accuracy. Brahmagupta (598-668) was the head of the astronomical observatory at Ujjain and during his tenure there, he wrote a text on astronomy, the Brahmasphutasiddhanta in 628.

Bhaskara (1114-1185) was the head of the astronomical observatory at Ujjain, continuing the mathematical tradition of Brahmagupta. He wrote the Siddhantasiromani which consists of two parts: Goladhyaya (sphere) and Grahaganita (mathematics of the planets).

The other important names of historical astronomers from India are Madhava and Nilakantha.

Aryabhatta's Magnum Opus, the Aryabhattiya was translated into Latin in the 13th century. Through this translation, European mathematicians got to know methods for calculating the areas of triangles, volumes of spheres as well as square and cube root. Aryabhatta's ideas about eclipses and the sun being the source of moonlight may not have caused much of an impression on European astronomers as by then they had come to know of these facts through the observations of Copernicus and Galileo.

Distance Between Sun and Earth

According to modern science, the Earth's orbit around the Sun is not perfectly circular but slightly elliptical. Therefore, the distance between the earth and the sun varies throughout the year.

At its nearest point on the ellipse, that is the earth's orbit around the sun, the earth is 91,445,000 miles (147,166,462 kms) from the sun. This point in the earth's orbit is known as Periapsis (perihelion) and it occurs around January 3.

The earth is farthest away from the sun around July 3 when it is 94,555,000 miles (152,171,522 km) from the sun. This point in the earth's orbit is called Apoapsis (aphelion).

The average distance from the earth to the sun is 92,955,807 miles (149,597,870.691 km).

According to Records, For the first time in 1672, Jean Richer and Giovanni Domenico Cassini measured the distance between Earth and Sun as 22,000 times of Earth Radii.(Earth's Radius is 6,371 Kms).

i.e 22000 x 6371 kms = 140,162,000 kms (140 Million Kms).

Two lines of Hindu Prayer "Hanuman Chalisa" computes this distance with great simplicity. This prayer was composed by Poet Tulasidas in the 15th century.

The prayer says:

yuga sahasra yojana para bhanu, lilyo tahi madhura phala janun
Translation is: Sun is at a distance of yuga Sahastra Yojanas.
According to Vedic conversion scales:
1 Yuga = 12000
1 Sahastra= 1000
1 Yojan = 8 Miles
Thus 12000 X 1000 X 8 = 96,000,000 miles
I mile = 1.6 kms
This further implies that distance is
96,000,000 * 1.6 kms = 153,600,000 Kms.

This is from a 15th century text in Awadhi dialect. This means even an ordinary villager in India knew finer intricacies of modern astronomy.

7.

Why Money?

Take Away The ATM Itself!

A man in Colorado, US, tried to steal an ATM by hauling it away with a stolen truck.

The plan didn't work. The attempted theft of the outdoor ATM in Boulder set off an alarm early morning. When police arrived they found the ATM on its side about 15 feet from its foundation outside a Chase Bank. No money had been taken.

Surveillance photos showed a man hooking the ATM's chain to the back of a U-Haul truck. The truck, which had been reported as stolen, was discovered a short distance away later that day.

Instead of stealing money from the ATM, the thief in question tried to steal the ATM itself. This is very similar to our story.

This world is an undisputed property of God because it existed before we came here and will continue to exist after we leave. We humans are trying to haul it away from its lawful owner, God. Instead of stealing resources of the world, we are trying to haul away the World itself. We are denying the hand of God by manufacturing philosophies like Darwinism or Big Bang and in the name of nationalism, we are trying to carve

out our share of the loot. We are also depriving other living beings their due share of natural resources.

Srila Prabhupada explains in a conversation, *"Tena tyaktena bhunjitha:* [Isopanisad mantra 1] everything belongs to God. Just like the father has got many sons and the father is the proprietor of the house. He gives one son, "This is your room," and the other son, "This is your room." So the obedient son is satisfied what the father allows to him. Others, those who are not obedient, they want to disturb the other brother that "This room also belongs to us." That creates chaos and confusion in the world. The United Nations, they have created a society for unity of the nations, but actually that is not unity. That is another way of encroaching upon others' property. Therefore there is no peace, unless they accept God is the Supreme proprietor. And we must be satisfied with the allotment God has given to us. Then there is no trouble. But the trouble is that we are not satisfied with the allotment given to us. That allotment can be understood by language or similar culture. So why one should encroach upon others' property which is allotted by God? That creates disturbance. So this so-called modern civilized man, first of all they create disturbances, and then they want to make some adjustment."

Modern man is also squandering rare natural resources, which are meant to be shared by all living beings, to fuel his insatiable greed. This greed manifests itself in the form of rampant consumerism.

By stealing from God we become subject to punishment by His police force, known as material nature. As soon as we use the property of God for unrestricted sense enjoyment, the nature inflicts

miseries upon us. World is a disturbed place because thieves can not be peaceful, being apprehensive of arrest always.

This global loot has set the burglar alarms ringing, only if we are willing to listen. Climatic change, food crisis, financial meltdowns, social unrest, resource depletion etc. are tintinnabulation of the very same alarm.

8.

Auschwitz Around Us

The Differential Treatment For Extra Two Legs

The train rumbled along in the dead of night and every one around was fast asleep. I was lying wide awake in my upper berth, reflecting on the darkness all around. Everyone slept soundly, surrendering their lives in the hands of the train driver and signal man. It was evident that surrender is an integral part of life and no one can live even for a moment without surrendering or having faith in some one. These people in their slumber were not concerned whether the train was on right track or whether the driver was drunk. They paid money to reserve a berth. In other words, they paid money to surrender their lives to the train personnel. Then, is God unreasonable in demanding our unconditional surrender, which we are already doing at every step of life?

Reflecting on the arrangements for comfort like air-conditioning, night lamp, sheets and blankets, my thoughts drifted towards travel arrangements for less priviledged beings

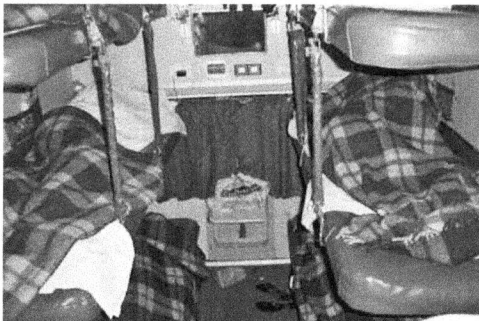

known as animals. The treatment for having extra two legs is markedly different.

The treatment meted out to these poor things, at least in India, is beyond the capacity of words to portray. After rendering a life time of service, these creatures are mercilessly loaded into trucks or railway wagons. This causes extensive injuries at the very onset of their journey. This is the beginning of their inglorious end. Their ordeal may last for days or weeks. They may be loaded or unloaded several

times. Injured, starved and thirsty, lucky ones pass way in transit itself. Others have to live through the ordeal much longer. At the time of unloading, they are thrown or dragged and left lying in open, awaiting their turn for slaughter. In great pain they await the arrival of merciful death.

As there are different ways to live, there are different ways to die also. Killing is one thing and killing by inflicting pain and torture is another. Srila Prabhupada explains: "In the Vedic civilization, meat-eaters are advised to kill an animal for the goddess Kali or a similar demigod. This is in order not to give the animal unnecessary pain, as slaughterhouses do. In the bali-dana sacrifice to a demigod, it is recommended to cut the throat of an animal with one slice. (Chaitanya Charitamrta, Madhya 24.250)

In the 16th century classic, Sri Chaitanya Charitamrta, there is a narration of the great sage Narada instructing a hunter who used to torture animals before killing.

> pathe ye sukara-mrga, jani tomara haya"
>
> vyadha kahe, -- "yei kaha, sei ta' niscaya"
>
> "'I was wondering whether all the boars and other animals that are half-killed belong to you.' "The hunter replied, 'Yes, what you are saying is so.'
>
> narada kahe, -- "yadi jive mara' tumi bana

ardha-mara kara kene, na lao parana?"

"Narada Muni then inquired, 'Why did you not kill the animals completely? Why did you half-kill them by piercing their bodies with arrows?'

vyadha kahe, -- "suna, gosani, 'mrgari' mora nama
pitara siksate ami kari aiche kama

"The hunter replied, 'My dear saintly person, my name is Mrgari, enemy of animals. My father taught me to kill them in that way.

ardha-mara jiva yadi dhad-phada kare
tabe ta' ananda mora badaye antare"

"'When I see half-killed animals suffer, I feel great pleasure.'

narada kahe, -- 'eka-vastu magi tomara sthane'
vyadha kahe, -- "mrgadi laha, yei tomara mane

"Narada Muni then told the hunter, 'I have one thing to beg of you.' "The hunter replied, 'You may take whatever animals or anything else you would like.

mrga-chala caha yadi, aisa mora ghare
yei caha taha diba mrga-vyaghrambare"

"'I have many skins, if you would like them. I shall give you either a deerskin or a tiger skin.'

narada kahe, -- "iha ami kichu nahi cahi
ara eka-dana ami magi toma-thani

"Narada Muni said, 'I do not want any of the skins. I am asking only one thing from you in charity.

kali haite tumi yei mrgadi mariba
prathamei mariba, ardha-mara na kariba"

"'I beg you that from this day on you will kill animals completely and not leave them half-dead.'

vyadha kahe, -- "kiba dana magila amare
ardha marile kiba haya, taha kaha more"

"The hunter replied, 'My dear sir, what are you asking of me? What is wrong with the animals' lying there half-killed? Will you please explain this to me?'

narada kahe, -- "ardha marile jiva paya vyatha
jive duhkha ditecha, tomara ha-ibe aiche avastha

"Narada Muni replied, 'If you leave the animals half-dead, you are purposefully giving them pain. Therefore you will have to suffer in retaliation.'

vyadha tumi, jiva mara -- 'alpa' aparadha tomara

kadarthana diya mara' -- e papa 'apara'

Narada Muni continued, 'My dear hunter, your business is killing animals. That is a slight offense on your part. But when you consciously give them unnecessary pain by leaving them half-dead, you incur very great sins.

(Chaitanya Charitamrta, Madhya 24.240-250)

9.

Surrendering Life

One Day At A Time

A young aspirant was walking with a senior, seasoned master in the garden one day. Feeling a bit insecure about what God had for him to do, he asked the master for some advice. The master walked up to a rosebush and handed the young aspirant a rosebud and told him to open it without tearing off any petals. The young aspirant looked in disbelief at the master and tried to figure out what a rosebud could possibly have to do with his wanting to know the will of God for his life and activities. But because of his great respect for the master, he proceeded to try to unfold the rose, while keeping every petal intact... It wasn't long before he realized how impossible this was to do. Noticing the young man's inability to

tam eva saranam gaccha
sarva-bhavena bharata
tat-prasadat param santim
sthanam prapsyasi sasvatam
 O scion of Bharata, surrender unto Him utterly. By His grace you will attain transcendental peace and the supreme and eternal abode. (*Bhagavad-gita 18.62*)

unfold the rosebud without tearing it, the master began to recite the following poem...

It is only a tiny rosebud,
A flower of God's design;
But I cannot unfold the petals,
With these clumsy hands of mine.
The secret of unfolding flowers,
Is not known to such as I.
God opens this flower so sweetly,
Then in my hands they die.
If I cannot unfold a rosebud,
This flower of God's design,
Then how can I have the wisdom,
To unfold this life of mine?
So I'll trust in God for leading,
Each moment of my day.
I will look to God for His guidance,
Each step of the way.
The pathway that lies before me,
Only God knows.
I'll trust Him to unfold the moments,
Just as He unfolds the rose.

"Therefore we shall fully surrender to Krsna. As Bhaktivinoda Thakura says, marobi rakhobi yo iccha tohara: "Now I surrender. Now if you want to maintain me, that is all right, and if You want to kill me, that is also all right." This is surrender. It is not business, "If You maintain me, then I surrender. If You kill me, then I do not." ~Srila Prabhupada (Morning Walk, May 2, 1974, Bombay)

10

Advancement of Civilization

Tempering With The Perfect Ways of God

One hot day, a traveller was taking it easy in the shade of a walnut tree. After a time, he started eying speculatively, the huge pumpkins growing on vines and the small walnuts growing on a majestic tree.

- Sometimes I just can't understand the ways of God! he mused. Just fancy letting tiny walnuts grow on so majestic a tree and huge pumpkins on the delicate vines!

Just then a walnut snapped off and fell smack on the traveller's bald head. He got up at once and lifting up his hands and face to heavens in supplication, said:

- Oh, my God! Forgive my questioning your ways! You are all-wise. Where would I have been now, if pumpkins grew on trees!

God's systems are perfect, man made systems are defective and dangerous.

11.

Olympic Games

More Animpic Than Humanpic

The World has just witnessed the great spectacle Olympics, an event synonymous with human triumph and achievement. This is the time to tune in, drop everything else to watch in awe as exuberant young bodies run, jump, lift and dive and as the news of medal tally pours in. The Olympics stir emotions like no other sporting event as athletes and fans are heartbroken or overjoyed.

But organizing an even of such scale is not easy. Great preparations mark the staging of this prestigious global event. Years before the event, architects and planners start racking their brains for erecting an 'Olympic city' which boasts gorgeous stadia and various other facilities for distinguished guests and athletes. Foolproof arrangements are made for accommodation, entertainment, medical care and of course, security. Many billions of dollars are spent in this historic endeavor by the hosting country.

Apart from the host, the participating nations also prepare and groom their athletes for years. Billions are spent in their training and equipments.

The Chinese Olympics was the most expensive sports event in human history, entailing a budget of over $48 billion. London, the next host for 2012 games, admits that it can't equal the scale and stature of the extravaganza in Beijing because the allocated budget is mere $18 billion.

And all this to check out who can run faster, who can jump higher, who can swim better and who can punch harder. But animals all around us can accomplish this much better, without spending billions and without any gorgeous arrangements.

And these billions can solve 'all' the world problems if spent wisely. Out of Beijing Olympic's 48 billion dollars, 40 billion dollars would have sufficed, according to UNHDR, to achieve universal access to basic social services in all developing countries:

Global Priority	$U.S. Billions
Basic education for all	6
Water and sanitation for all	9
Reproductive health for all women	12
Basic health and nutrition	13

(Source: The state of human development, United Nations Human Development Report 1998, Chapter 1, p.37)

Therefore mismanagement of the world resources in the real cause of all our problems.

Olympic motto is 'Citius altius fortius' or faster, higher and stronger. But it should not mean running faster or jumping higher or stronger muscles. A dog can easily outrun the fastest athlete, a kangaroo can jump higher than any world champion and an elephant can lift several weight lifters along with the weights they are struggling to lift.

Srila Prabhupada summarizes this in the phrase, *bahvarambhe laghu kriya.* "You can make a very high-grade arrangement, but the result is zero... They do not know what is spiritual life, what is ultimate goal. Simply like cats and dogs. The dog jumps over with

four legs, and if a man can jump over with four wheels, then that is advancement. Just see....again they have made this car, coming from miles away, but the business is fishing. Just see. *Bambharambhe laghu-kriya*. "Advancement of civilization, we have got car, we are nicely dressed, we are human being, everything..." But what is our business? Fishing. ... Arambha, gorgeous arrangement -- the business is the same. The skylark, what is called? Skylark? These birds?... seagulls. They are also doing the same business, and after his much advancement of civilization, he is doing the same business. The tiger is also eating flesh and blood, and human being -- a scientific slaughterhouse. The same business, but they have got scientific instrument how to cut the throat quickly. This is the advancement of

civilization. The dog and cat they are having sex on the open street, and now they are talking of homosex in the schools, colleges for education. This is their position. They do not know even what is the standard of human civilization. If you are doing the same business like ordinary animals, then where is the advancement of civilization? (Morning Walk -- May 11, 1975, Perth)

One World, One Dream - Countless hypocrisies

The official motto for the Beijing Olympics was 'One World, One Dream.' Of course restrictions Apply. Tibet Not Included."

At a recent press conference, a reporter asked the chairman of the Chinese Olympic Committee about China's Olympic slogan, "One world, one dream."

"As recently as ten years ago," said the reporter, "Chinese leaders expressed their plans to spread Communism throughout the world by the use of force. How do you respond to critics who believe the 'one world' idea in the Olympic slogan sounds like a plan for world conquest?"

"That's ridiculous," said the Chinese spokesman. " One world simply refers to the fact that the entire world is gathering together in Beijing for the Olympics. It's a statement of unity. Any suggestion that China is trying to conquer the world is absurd."

"And what about the 'one dream' part of the slogan?" asked the reporter. "What is the dream?"

"A society founded on Marxist principles, of course," came the reply.

China announced that during the Olympics, protesters will be allowed to assemble in designated protest areas or, as they're commonly called in China, jails.

The dream of one world can not be realized by holding Olympics. Olympics will go on and wars will go on. Peace and unity is only possible on spiritual platform as suggested by Sripad Sankaracharya twelve centuries ago:

ekam sastram devaki-putra-gitam

eko devo devaki-putra eva

eko mantras tasya namani yani

karmapy ekam tasya devasya seva

"In this present day, people are very much eager to have one scripture, one God, one religion, and one occupation. Therefore, *ekam sastram devaki-putra-gitam*: let there be one scripture only, one common scripture for the whole world - Bhagavad-gita. *Eko devo devaki-putra eva*: let there be one God for the whole world- Sri Krsna. *Eko mantras tasya namani*: and one hymn, one mantra, one prayer -- the chanting of His name: *Hare Krsna, Hare Krsna, Krsna Krsna, Hare Hare/ Hare Rama, Hare Rama, Rama Rama, Hare Hare. Karmapy ekam tasya devasya seva*: and let there be one work only -- the service of the Supreme Personality of Godhead."

(Srila Prabhupada, Bhagavad-gita Introduction)

A Humanpics Manifesto

Human society is becoming frivolous. People are less serious about higher values in life like character and integrity. Whole mood is to take life very lightly and do your own thing without any standard code of conduct. Trivialities are vying for more attention than ever before.

Srila Bhaktisiddhanta Sarasvati Thakura used to say, "There is no scarcity of anything within this world. The only scarcity is of Krsna consciousness." Enough resources have been provided by God for all the residents of this planet to live happily but there is gross mismanagement as far as distribution is concerned. Lavish spendings in countless frivolous engagements like recently held games would be one such example.

Humanpic Events

In Olympics, the athletes compete in dozens of events like archery, athletics, badminton, basketball, boxing, cycling, diving, hockey, sailing, shooting and swimming. But may be the International Olympic Committee should consider adding some events which would bring out the finer traits of human personality. In activities of Jumping, running, swimming or punching, animals excel us in every possible way.

Therefore, besides Aquatics, some athletes can compete in event known as austerity or self-control because this is the foremost function of human life. Champions in this category are too numerous to mention and vedic literature known as Srimad Bhagavatam is filled with examples of record holders in this category.

Hockey is good but better still is hearing about God. By hearing about God, we accomplish the prime purpose of human life. In one 'humanpic' held long ago, King Pariksit is said to have won the gold in this category.

In place of or along with cycling, let there be an event called 'care for other life forms'. King Pariksit won the gold medal by protecting an innocent cow from the hands of an unscrupulous low class man.

Gymnastics would go well along with 'Glorification of God' because after all this is what differentiates mankind from dogkind. From Sukadeva Goswami to Srila Prabhupada, thousands have won gold in this series throughout the ages.

Another area different countries could possibly compete is 'Chanting the holy name'. Haridas Thakura is an all time legend in this game.

How about 'Truthfulness' along side with Table tennis? King Yudhisthir was one such titleholder.

If there is Weightlifting, why not add the event called, 'Word of honor'. This game would make an interesting show in this age of lying and deceit. Previous gold medalists are Maharaja Dasarath and Bali.

Some other categories could be renunciation, knowledge of religious principles, charity, sacrifice, compassion etc.

There are hundreds of sporting events like this which are worth competing for by human beings and which would testify human excellence in its true sense.

12.

Blessed Crows

And Cursed Cows

It was a quiet night in the rustic town of Vrindavan. The utter silence of night was broken by barking of dogs and monkeys screeching on rooftops. Cows were lying down in the potholed alleys. At this hour, they didn't have to worry about recklessly driven vehicles. Then there was intermittent cooing of peacocks. It was all quiet and calm with townsfolk in deep slumber.

Suddenly, the whole neighborhood was stirring up in commotion with rumbling trucks, men rushing about and cows wailing. Subhangi Devi Dasi, a resident from overseas, was woken up to witness a sight none of us would ever dream could be happening in this holy place. Krishna's cows were being violently kidnapped in the night. It is believed the cows are killed and sold for their flesh and leather products.

Arjuna, one of the men trying to protect a cow shelter says the kidnappers came with several trucks. "They caught and stole 48 cows just here in this area. The men were ruthless, throwing the cows in the back of their trucks, beating then and in some cases killing them if they were resisting. Blood was everywhere."

Villagers say the kidnappers are always armed and attack anyone who tries to stop them. "A month or so back," Arjuna says, "the police put up barricades to try to stop the kidnappers. That night they rammed the barricades with their trucks."

"It is so out of control," says Arjuna. "Vrindavan is the land of cows and these demons have become aware that there are so many cows and goshallas just ripe for the picking." The locals are helpless. They can do little without risking their own lives.

It is reported that 15 days ago, when the police tried to stop them, the kidnappers rammed a police jeep. A policeman fired a shot and he got a rock in the head for his effort. It is reported that the police had to pull back as there were only four of them, whilst there were eight heavily armed kidnappers. "The criminals seem to be aware of how much resistance they will encounter and come prepared to meet it." Arjuna says.

"Sometimes they hit the cows in the head with rocks and sometimes shoot them or hack them with machetes if they resist," says Arjuna. "They used to come in one truck now they travel with four trucks at a time."

Subhangi Devi Dasi says she has heard the cows can fetch up to 10,000 rupees. It is no wonder kidnappers are armed and are prepared to injure even the police. Villagers who try to prevent the kidnappings are said to be placing themselves and their families in a dangerous situation.

People have contacted the authorities but to no avail. Even the chief minister of the state has been approached but apparently she is busy with erecting her statues. Even police seems to be hand in gloves with the rustlers because they appear to be pretending their efforts to stop them. Residents feel that just a handful of rustlers,

> The age of Kali means mismanagement and quarrel. And the root cause of all mismanagement and quarrel is that worthless men with the modes of lower-class men, who have no higher ambition in life, come to the helm of the state management. Such men at the post of a king are sure to first hurt the cow and the brahminical culture, thereby pushing all society towards hell. Maharaja Pariksit, trained as he was, got the scent of this root cause of all quarrel in the world. Thus he wanted to stop it in the very beginning.
>
> ~ Srimad Bhagavatam (1.16.4)

unless supported by the administration, can not hold entire towns to ransom.

Protecting innocent animals, especially cows, is a prime governmental duty. These animals are also nationals as they have taken birth in the country.

On one hand, all complaints to the concerned department have fallen on deaf ears, on the other government is indiscriminately issuing licenses for new slaughterhouses and even providing subsidies.

Srimad Bhagavatam states,

stri-bala-go-dvija-ghnas ca
para-dara-dhanadrtah
uditasta-mita-praya
alpa-sattvalpakayusah

asamskrtah kriya-hina
rajasa tamasavrtah
prajas te bhaksayisyanti
mleccha rajanya-rupinah

These barbarians in the guise of kings will devour the citizenry, murdering innocent women, children, cows and brahmanas and coveting the wives and property of other men. They will be erratic in their moods, have little strength of character and be very short-lived. Indeed, not purified by any Vedic rituals and lacking in the practice of regulative principles, they will be completely covered by the modes of passion and ignorance. ~ *Srimad Bhagavatam (12.1.39-40)*

This is the position of cows in the state of Uttar Pradesh. But crows are having better times. Uttar Pradesh government is going out of its way to provide them perching pedestals and toilet stands. Over Rs. 3000 crores (700 million USD) of public money has been spent to erect the statues of the chief minister and her party symbol in what is India's most deprived state. This statue mania has irked even the apex court which has issued notices to the state government questioning this wasteful expenditure. Union home minister has condemned the move, "Thousands of crores are being spent on establishing statues of elephants and herself. Can there be something more shameful than this in Indian politics. Of what use will be the statues in UP. These crores could have helped wipe out poverty of thousands of people, provide basic amenities and education."

At the time of writing of this article, in one week alone she has unveiled 15 new memorials. And there are no indications

---

prsadhras tu manoh putro
go-palo guruna krtah
palayam asa ga yatto
ratryam virasana-vratah

Among these sons, Prsadhra, following the order of his spiritual master, was engaged as a protector of cows. He would stand all night with a sword to give the cows protection.

One who becomes virasana takes the vow to stand all night with a sword to give protection to the cows. Because Prsadhra was engaged in this way, it is to be understood that he had no dynasty. We can further understand from this vow accepted by Prsadhra how essential it is to protect the cows. Some son of a ksatriya would take this vow to protect the cows from ferocious animals, even at night. What then is to be said of sending cows to slaughterhouses? This is the most sinful activity in human society.

~Srimad Bhagavatam 9.2.3

this statue fetish will be given up sometime soon. Each statue of the leader costs a sum of Rs 6.65 crores and each elephant statue costs more than Rs 70 lakh. In addition, hundreds of crores have been spent on developing and landscaping these memorial sites. Another hundreds of crores will be spent annually to maintain these sites. All this money being spent in a state where over 60% of the population defecates in open.

I loved Venice: So many statues to perch upon and people to feed you...

According to latest revelations, these larger-than-life statues may have been built upon outsized corruption. The new chief minister says the statues may encircle a 40,000 crore scam.

The economic offences wing of the state's Criminal Investigation Department (CID) is attempting to figure out who benefited from the alleged scam.

130 statues of huge elephants, placed in parks in Noida and Lucknow should have cost only Rs. 5 lakh but were bought by a state-run agency for 60 lakhs each.

13.

Beads In Hands

Or Tags On Legs

Demigods want to take birth in India and those who have taken birth in India want to go to America.

In the upper planetary systems, all roads lead to India as stated by 'all the' demigods in Srimad Bhagavatam:

"Since the human form of life is the sublime position for spiritual realization, all the demigods in heaven speak in this way: How wonderful it is for these human beings to have been born in the land of Bharata-varsa. They must have executed pious acts of austerity in the past, or the Supreme Personality of Godhead Himself must have been pleased with them. Otherwise, how could they engage in devotional service in so many ways? We demigods can only aspire to achieve human births in Bharata-varsa to execute devotional service, but these human beings are already engaged there." (Srimad Bhagavatam 5.19.21)

But in India, all roads lead to America, even if it means getting animal tags. Last year hundreds of Indian students enrolled in various programmes at Tri-Valley University were RFID-tagged (radio frequency identification) so as to keep track of their movements by the US federal authorities. These microchip-embedded tags are used for animals like cats and dogs so that they don't go missing.

Tri-Valley University, according to a federal complaint filed in a California court, was raided and shut down for helping foreign nationals illegally acquire immigration status.

When Indian media published photos of Indian students with the humiliating tags around their feet, Indian government objected. The US government summed up its response in five words, "This is a standard procedure." Human Rights supporters have called the move "degrading and inhuman."

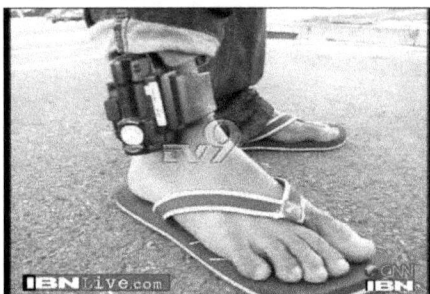

But when Indians, who are meant to give spiritual knowledge to the world, go begging in the name of technological education, such humiliation is not very surprising. In fact, Indians overseas don't enjoy a very high reputation due to a general lack of scruples. Srila Prabhupada, a spiritual master from India also went to America but not to beg but to give 'something substantial'. He had a piece of advice for Indian students overseas:

"So if, those who are Indians, especially present in this meeting, that if you want to glorify your country, then you present this Vedic literature. You cannot excel the western countries by so-called technological knowledge. That is not possible. They are far advanced. Hundred years advance. Whatever machine you may discover, that machine was discovered one hundred years ago in western countries. So you cannot. Anything. So if you want, Indians, to glorify your country, then present this Vedic culture heart and soul, and Just like I am trying to do it. So how people are accepting it? There is substance. Before me so many swamis came in this country, they could not present the real thing. They wanted some money and went away. That's all. Our, this Krsna consciousness movement is not that. We want to give something to the western countries. That is our purpose. We have not come to beg, we have come to give them something. That is my mission. They come here to beg, "Give me rice, give me dahl, give me wheat, give me money," but I have come here to give something of Indian culture. That is the difference."(Lecture, New York, July 6, 1972)

India is supposed to be a special place due to facilities it offers for spiritual development. Also birth in India is supposed to be a special privilege available only to a selected few. For Indians opting for western ways, it's an opportunity lost. Demigods in heavenly planets glorify Bharata-varsa, India as mentioned in 5th Canto of Srimad Bhagavatam.

The demigods continue: After performing the very difficult tasks of executing Vedic ritualistic sacrifices, undergoing austerities, observing vows and giving charity, we have achieved this position as inhabitants of the heavenly planets. But what is the value of this achievement? Here we are certainly very engaged in material sense gratification, and therefore we can hardly remember the lotus feet of Lord Narayana. Indeed, because of our excessive sense gratification, we have almost forgotten His lotus feet. (Srimad Bhagavatam 5.19.22)

A short life in the land of Bharata-varsa is preferable to a life achieved in Brahmaloka for millions and billions of years because even if one is elevated to Brahmaloka, he must return to repeated birth and death. Although life in Bharata-varsa, in a lower planetary system, is very short, one who lives there can elevate himself to full Krsna consciousness and achieve the highest perfection, even in this short life, by fully surrendering unto the lotus feet of the Lord. Thus one attains Vaikunthaloka, where there is neither anxiety nor repeated birth in a material body. (Srimad Bhagavatam 5.19.23)

An intelligent person does not take interest in a place, even in the topmost planetary system, if the pure Ganges of topics concerning the Supreme Lord's activities does not flow there, if there are not devotees engaged in service on the banks of such a river of piety, or if there are no festivals of sankirtana-yajna to satisfy the Lord [especially since sankirtana-yajna is recommended in this age]. (Srimad Bhagavatam 5.19.24)

Bharata-varsa offers the proper land and circumstances in which to execute devotional service, which can free one from the results of jnana and karma. If one obtains a human body in the land of Bharata-varsa, with clear sensory organs with which to execute the sankirtana-yajna, but in spite of this opportunity he does not take to devotional service, he is certainly like liberated forest animals and birds that are careless and are therefore again bound by a hunter. (*Srimad Bhagavatam* 5.19.25)

We are now living in the heavenly planets, undoubtedly as a result of our having performed ritualistic ceremonies, pious activities and yajnas and having studied the Vedas. However, our lives here will one day be finished. We pray that at that time, if any merit remains from our pious activities, we may again take birth in Bharata-varsa as human beings able to remember the lotus feet of the Lord. The Lord is so kind that He personally comes to the land of Bharata-varsa and expands the good fortune of its people.

(*Srimad Bhagavatam* 5.19.28)

14.

Dogocracy

My name is Duncan MacDonald and I live in Washington State. My mistress Jane Balogh registered me to vote and submitted ballots in my name in September and November 2006 and May 2007 elections. She used a paw print to mark ballots on my behalf.

She has been charged with misdemeanor of making false statements on a voter registration form and faces a maximum sentence of 90 days in jail and a $1,000 fine.

As a shepherd-terrier of a respectable descent, I think I need to speak out. I have many suppressed feelings and it is not good to keep things bottled up. As you all know, my species is a very patient one but I feel greatly humiliated that simply for putting my name in voter's list, my mistress may have to go to jail. What is so bad about us and what is so great about you all. You voters (and for that matter your leaders) are no better off.

In this controversy, what needs to be examined is whether modern voters (and for that matter, their leaders) are any better off than cats and dogs. To call a human being a dog might be an insult and so would be to call us a human being.

Aren't we four legged animals more humane and warmhearted? Do we ever rob, lie, cheat, rape, drop atom bombs or kill babies in the womb? Do we ever indulge in arson, bribery, burglary or child abuse? Did any one hear of us doing pornography, credit card fraud, domestic violence or drug trafficking? Where are the hate crimes, extortion, kidnapping, prostitution or racketeering in our society? And do we ever seek enjoyment in others suffering? Who is more humane of the two? Where is the humanity in you, the two-legged animals?

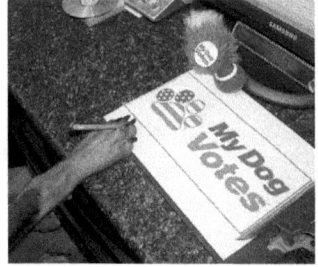

I feel to call you people 'human' is a misuse of the word. What you two-legged animals have achieved in all these years other than destroying the planet, destroying life and destroying your ownselves. Shouldn't you take lessons from us, the honest and unpretentious creatures, on how to live, behave and work.

There is a saying.

If you can start the day without caffeine or pep pills

If you can be cheerful, ignoring aches and pains,

If you can resist complaining and boring people with you troubles,

If you can eat the same food everyday and be grateful for it,

If you can understand when loved ones are too busy to give you time,

If you can overlook when people take things out on you, when through no fault of your, something goes wrong,

If you can take criticism and blame without resentment,

If you can face the world without lies and deceit,

If you can conquer tension without medical help,

If you can relax without liquor,

If you can sleep without the aid of drugs,

Then, you are almost as good as your dog.

What Separates Mankind From Dogkind

ahara-nidra-bhaya-maithunam ca
samanyam etat pasubhir naranam
dharmo hi tesam adhiko viseso
dharmena hinah pasubhih samanah

Eating, sleeping, sex and defense, these four principles are common to both human beings and dogs. The distinction between human life and dog life is that a human being can search after God but a dog cannot. That is the difference. Therefore a man without the urge to search after God is no better than a dog. *(Hitopadesh)*

Srila Prabhupada explains: "The dog is eating according to his nature, and we are also eating, but in a nice place, with nicely cooked food on a nice table, that is not advancement. The principle is still eating. Similarly, you may sleep in a very nice apartment in a six-story building or in a 122-story building, and the dog may lie in a street, but when he sleeps and when you sleep, there is no difference. You cannot know whether you are sleeping in a skyscraper or on the ground because you are dreaming something which has taken you from your bed. You have forgotten that your body is lying there on the bed, and you are flying in the air, dreaming. Therefore, to improve the sleeping method is not advancement of civilization. Similarly, the dog has no social custom for mating. Whenever there is a she-dog, he mates on the street. You may mate very silently, in a secret place (although now people are learning how to mate like dogs), but the mating is there. The same principle applies to defending. A dog has teeth and nails with which he can defend himself, and you have atom bombs. But the purpose is defending, that's all."

When two puppies were fighting and mother dog enquired. "He called me the son of a woman" replied one of the puppies.

The Dogs Hold An Election

Once a long time ago, the dogs were trying to elect a president. So one of them got up in the big dog convention and said: "I nominate the bulldog for president.

He's strong. He can fight."

"But he can't run," said another dog. "What good is a fighter who can't run?

So some one nominated a airedale terrier.

But the other dogs cried: "Naw, he can run all right, but he can't fight. When he catches up with somebody, what happens then? He gets the hell beaten out of him, that's what! So all he good for is running away."

Then an ugly little mutt jumped up and said: "I nominate that dog for president who has a straight tail."

And immeditatley an equally ugly mutt jumped up and said: "I second the motion."

At once all the dogs started checking out each other's tails. A big chorus went up:

"Oh no, he does not have a straight tail."

"No, neither does this one."

"He's no presidential timber!"

"No, he no good, either."

"This one sure isn't the people's choice."

"Wow, this ain't my candidate!"

They're still looking for a good leader, and still haven't found him.

And neither have we.

In Normal, IL., it is against the law to make faces at dogs.

15.

World Toilet Summit

Progress of Human Civilization

In The Art of Defecating

The World Toilet Summit – 2007 was organized by Government of India, World Toilet Organisation (Singapore) and some NGOs in New Delhi from October 31 to November 3, 2007. In this summit, 150 distinguished scholars, academics, economists and leaders from 44 countries participated. This Summit provided a forum to exchange ideas, discuss strategies and sanitation technologies suitable for different countries, climes and cultures. It sought to produce a synthesis of knowledge and experiences and evolve a common view on how best to achieve the Millennium Development Goal on Sanitation by 2015. It was also organized to build a global alliance towards this end.

Dr. A.P.J. Abdul Kalam, former President of India, inaugurated the Summit.

HRH Willem-Alexander, the Prince of Orange of the Netherlands and Chairman of the United Nations Secretary-General's Advisory Board on Water and Sanitation, spoke at length on the urgency to provide toilets to 1.2 billion people in the world to meet the

Millennium Development Goal. He praised the Government of India for showing tremendous efforts in its Total Sanitation Campaign. "Their efforts are truly laudable and I feel really proud and honoured to be a part of this programme," said the Prince. He even suggested organizing a similar show at the United Nations to turn the spotlight on the issue of toilets. He ended his inspiring speech by quoting Mahatma Gandhi "Be the change you want to see in the world." Dr. Raghuvansh Prasad Singh, Mrs. Meira Kumar, Kumari Selja, Prof. K.J. Nath and Mr. Jack Sim addressed the seminar.

Seldom before so many distinguished persons had gathered together, united in their concern to create a healthy world. By sheer weight of number of the people they represented and the experience that they brought along in the areas of toilets, the seventh World Toilet Summit became a memorable event.

The Expo at the World Toilet Summit 2007 had state-of-the-art toilet units with their jazzy colours and flashy interiors attracting visitors' attention. The manufacturers of these dream contraptions gathered at the Expo Toilet Summit to display their latest designs.

Reference:

http://news.bbc.co.uk/2/hi/7070494.stm

sulabhinternational.org

Does this function of answering nature's call require such international expertise so as to form a 'World Toilet Organization' with the head office in Singapore. Do all other species of life, moving and non-moving, not execute this function, without the need for all this 'expertise'. "The summit will be an excellent meeting opportunity for the exchange of information, ideas and know-how with international experts on toilet-related topics," declares the news release.

So this is all about the progress of human society in performing its animalistic functions in a more polished way. It is as if 'under-developed' people of past did not know how to use washroom. Now they are civilized and they are doing it in a scientific, advanced way. In fact, there is no scientific, advanced way of passing waste matter from the body. There can be no advanced or elegant way of doing it. Passing stool is what it is - passing stool, nothing more, nothing less.

Of course we have a problem in hand. According to a BBC report (31 Oct, 2007), In India more than 700 million people have no access to toilets. According to a World Bank report (Nov 19, 2013), 53 percent of Indian households defecate in open. That is the highest number of people in the world without access to toilet facilities.

It is a sight familiar to anyone travelling around India by train. Early morning, many Indian villagers head to the nearest railway track and squat by its side relieving themselves. Others use their fields, the forests or any piece of open land that they can find.

Is it so because India is a poor country? If India is a poor country, what about its black money outflow running into billions? Total black money outflow from India was nearly $343 billion (nearly Rs. 21 lakh crore) during 2002-2011, says the report titled 'Illicit Financial Flows from Developing Countries: 2002-2011'.

According to the same report, In 2011 alone, India suffered black money outflow of $84.93 billion (nearly Rs. 5 lakh crore). A very tiny portion of this money can solve this staggering problem of toilets. Incidentally, in last few decades, Trillions of dollars have been siphoned off and deposited in the safe heavens of Swiss banking systems while millions died of malnutrition and hunger back home.

Swiss Banking Association report. 2008, gives a break up of countrywise deposits. Here are the top 5 countries.

India—- $1,456 billion
Russia —$ 470 billion
UK ——-$390 billion
Ukraine – $100 billion
China —-$ 96 billion
Source: Swiss Banking Association report 2008

This is more money than all the money in all the banks in India taken together. There is more Indian money in Swiss banks than rest of the world combined.

Is India a poor country? An amount 13 times larger than the country's foreign debt stashed away in secret Swiss accounts, one needs to rethink if India is a poor country. This ill-begotten wealth is even higher than India's GDP and three times that of market capitalisation on national stock exchange.

So here we see that really there is no problem. God has provided sufficient resources for all living beings to live happily and peacefully. It is only a problem of maldistribution of resources. We, in the name of progress, have created these problems.

Srila Prabhupada explains: Even a small bird, he has arrangement for eating, he has arrangement for sleeping, he has arrangement for defending, and he has arrangement for mating. As soon as a bird is born, two eggs are born: one male, one female. That means from the beginning of his life, the mating problem is solved. There is no necessity. A bird, they never, the birds or beasts, they never seek, the male is seeking after female or female after seeking. That is automatically solved. Similarly, their eating is already there, and their sleeping accommodation is already there. So these are not problems, but we have created problems only for these four demands of the body. So Vedanta-sutra says that "Don't be busy about these problems." *Visayah khalu sarvatah syat*: "These problems are satisfied in any form of life." Why in human form? They have developed consciousness. They have got better business. Why they should be engaged only for these four principles of life? Huh? Their problem is to inquire, "What is the source of all these manifestations?"

Athato brahma jijnasa. The Vedanta-sutra informs, "Now you should inquire. You have got this developed consciousness of life, human form of life, very intelligent, and you are simply wasting your time simply for this eating,

sleeping and mating? Oh, this is not your only business.
(Lecture, Bhagavad-gita 9.13 -- New York, November 28, 1966)

It is interesting to note that other than "civilized" human beings, no other life form has this global crisis of toilets.

-There are over 800 million insects for every human on the planet.

-There are over 30 million mammals for every human on the planet.

-There are close to 100 trillion fish and acquatics in the ocean

-Globally ant population is expected to be around 4 quadrillion (A quadrillion is a 1 plus 15 zeros)

-Elephant population all over the world is 7,00,000. (It was 9 million 80 years ago)

None of these living beings have toilet issues and none of them have ever held a World Summit on this subject.

People have been answering the calls of nature since time immemorial. And it is not just a human prerogative. Eating, sleeping, sex, and defense these four principles are common to both human beings and animals. The distinction between human life and animal life is that a man can search after God but an animal cannot. That is the difference. Therefore a man without that urge for searching after God is no better than an animal.

Since eating is common to all species of life, evacuation is also a common function. Even trees and plants eat and evacuate in their own way. They are called 'padapa' in Sanskrit, meaning those who eat and drink through legs.

All these life forms have their toiletiquette without any training. The author saw a feral cat walk into their backyard, digup the place, do the thing and cover the ground back with dirt neatly, before walking away.

No education, no expertise is required to execute this gut function. Even a mosquito has expertise in this regard. In fact, animals, insects, reptiles and birds would seem to be more advanced than us because they are able to perform this activity without so much hassle and expenditure...and without the need for holding a 'World Summit'.

Bathroom Is A Room Too - Proliferation of Designer Bathrooms

The Expo at the World Toilet Summit 2007 had "state-of-the-art toilet units with their jazzy colours and flashy interiors attracting visitors' attention. The manufacturers of these dream contraptions gathered at the Expo Toilet Summit to display their designs."

No matter how much you decorate a bathroom, the quality of what you do there remains the same. This remains a place to quickly finish the rituals and get out. This world has been compared to a public toilet in Vedas. No matter how much you spray the perfume, a public restroom is never going to become a nice place. Wise man Chankya quotes in one place: "The anus can not become a pure organ however much you may wash it." Similarly the bathroom can never become a 'place to be' however much you may decorate it. It will remain what it is - a place to finish off your ablutions and get out.

Many a people have been drawn into the lure of designer bathrooms and they have ended up spending more on it than they can really afford. In some cases, people had their houses auctioned when they were unable to pay up the debts thus incurred. In eastern India there is a saying *"garib manus to jhinga khai, hakte gelo gauda jaya."* A poor man is able to eat only poor quality grasshoppers but while going to anwer the call of nature, he rides a regal horse.

In a designer restroom, the quality of stool does not change in any way. A gorgeous toilet does not make the excrement any more fragrant or acceptable than those passed in less luxurious settings. Its filth, no matter how much you aggrandize it.

When people completely lose sight of the goal of human life, they become preoccupied with animalistic activities. Advancement of civilization does not mean how to pass stool in a sophisticated manner but to develop higher faculties of human life.

Though India may be very eager to catchup with the 'in vogue' trends, China is ahead of her. A southwestern Chinese city, Chongqing, is 'flush with pride' in where a recently-opened porcelain palace features an Egyptian facade, soothing music and more than 1,000 toilets spread out over 32,290 square feet. Officials are preparing to submit an application to Guinness World Records to have the free four-story public bathroom listed as the world's largest." We are spreading toilet culture. People can listen to gentle music and watch TV. After they use the bathroom they will be very, very happy." says an official.

One Of The Highest Pleasures

In one sense the Chinese are correct when they say people using their designer toilets will be "very very happy". Relieving oneself is indeed one of the two top pleasures found in this material world. Srila Prabhupada narrates a story to this effect.

One day, A king's wife gave birth to a male child and the king was rejoicing. At that moment, the court jester, Gopala Bhan came into the room and the king said, "Gopala, on this very, very happy occasion, please tell me, what do you have to say? Tell me exactly how you feel at this moment."

Gopala replied, "Frankly, at this moment, I feel as happy as after passing stool."

When the world becomes degraded, civilization becomes demoniac, and for the common man the rectum and the genital are taken very seriously as the centers of all activity.
-Srila Prabhupada (Srimad Bhagavatam 4.29.14p)

"Gopala! How could you say such a thing?" The king was mortified. "On this auspicious moment, that's all you have to say? I am completely disgusted. It's not funny and I don't appreciate your humor at all."

After that, the relations between the king and Gopala were strained for some time. One day, Gopala was rowing the king down the river when the king suddenly had an urgent call of nature. Gopala said, "On this side there is a very heavy jungle area. It's not very suitable. Let us go a little further down and we'll find a better place."

The king said, "Go over to the side!"

Gopala said, "Not here. There is danger. Some thieves and dacoits. Your life may be endangered. There's a place ahead."

The king said, "Gopala, I cannot wait any longer. Immediately go over!" Gopala had to go over and the king jumped out. He could hardly contain himself. When the king returned, Gopala asked him, "How are you feeling?"

The king replied, "I am feeling very happy after passing stool."

Then Gopala said, "Don't you remember? This was exactly the situation I was in after your child was born. When you asked me at that moment what exactly I was feeling, I was in the same situation as you are now. I told you how I was feeling, but you thought I was insulting your son and you never appreciated it. Now do you understand?"

Cleanliness Is Next to Godliness

Of course it does not mean that basic sanitation is not required. The vedic culture attaches highest importance to cleanliness. Cleanliness is regarded as next to godliness. In fact it designates those who are clean as 'suchi' or brahmanas, and based on this qualification of cleanliness, internal and external, they were posted on the highest rung of social structure. Vedic toiletiquette is more complex as it enjoins taking a full bath rather than a light paper wipe. Great sages lived in forests without designer toilets but they presented a great deal of transcendental knowledge for the benefit of human society.

Today only 32% of Indians have access to the luxury of lavatories, rest of the population makes use of vast country side. Long ago, it was not so and India was better off in those days, as far as basic amenities of life were concerned. In February 1835, Lord MClau, a British Colonial wrote:

"I have traveled across the length and breath of India and I have not seen one person who is a beggar, who is a thief, such wealth I have seen in this country, such high moral values, people of such caliber (of noble character), that I do not think we would ever conquer this country .....unless we break the very backbone of this nation which is her spiritual and cultural heritage."

To conclude, it is interesting to see that human society is striving hard to improvise bathroom life but we wish the same amount of attention was given to develop higher human faculties also.

Srimad Bhagavatam (11.9.29) states:

labdhva sudurlabham idam bahu-sambhavante
manusyam arthadam anityam apiha dhirah
turnam yateta na pated anumrtyu yavan
nihsreyasaya visayah khalu sarvatah syat

"This human form of life is obtained after many, many births, and although it is not permanent, it can offer the highest benefits. Therefore a sober and intelligent man should immediately try to fulfill his mission and attain the highest profit in life before another death occurs. He should avoid sense gratification, which is available in all circumstances."

Conclusion

Srila Prabhupada says:

"Modern civilization is supposed to be making advancement in scientific knowledge, but what is this scientific knowledge? It is based on bodily comforts only, without knowledge that however comfortably one maintains his body, the body is destructible."

"Advancement of knowledge for eating, sleeping and mating is animal knowledge. A dog also knows how to eat, how to sleep, how to mate and how to defend. If our education extends only to these points, we are no better than animals. Therefore, scripture says that human life is not meant only for these four principles of life, bodily demands. There is another thing a human being should be inquisitive to learn what is Absolute Truth. That education is lacking."

"Advancement of civilization means advancement of the process of eating, advancement of the process of sleeping, advancement of process of sex life, advancement of defense. That's all. But that will not help us. Just like there are thieves. There were some thieves. They have got very organized system of stealing. Very educated, scientists, they can enter into the bank safety room. With scientific method, they can open the chest, treasury, and take, at a time, millions of dollars away. And there is another kind of thief, they simply pickpocket or burglar when they get opportunity, take away some goods from your house. In Hindi, it is called hira and khira. Somebody is stealing hira. Khira means cucumber. And somebody's stealing from your box hira. Hira means diamond. But if these two classes of thieves are arrested, according to law, they both are punishable."

"Similarly, if you become an advanced, civilized man simply to make a gorgeous scheme of this eating, sleeping, mating, and defending, you remain animal. These things they cannot understand. This rascal civilization, they think this is advancement of civilization. They cannot think that this advancement of civilization of industry, big, big cities, electric light, big, big road, motorcars and... But what is the basic principle? The basic principle is eating, sleeping, mating and defending. Just like the basic principle being stealing, you are thieves. Either you are expert thief for stealing diamonds or you are not expert, but you can steal one apple or one peach, both of you are thieves. So you are punishable. You are punished. The gorgeous thief, scientifically stealing from the bank millions of dollars, he cannot say that "I am advanced thief. In a very civilized way I take, at a time, millions of dollars. Therefore, my stealing is advancement of civilization." These rascals, they cannot understand this. Therefore we call all of them rascals. They may say that "We are so much advanced. The law is either you are advanced thief, or you are a crude thief, you are thief, and as soon as you are thief, you are punishable. This is the process."

"That is the defect of modern civilization. They are going to hell, and they're thinking they're advanced. This is the defect. *Adanta-gobhir visatam tamisram punah punas carvita-carvananam.*" [SB 7.5.30]. (From Lectures)

THE AUTHOR

Dr. Sahadeva dasa (Sanjay Shah) is a monk in vaisnava tradition. His areas of work include research in Vedic and contemporary thought, Corporate and educational training, social work and counselling, travelling, writing books and of course, practicing spiritual life and spreading awareness about the same.

He is also an accomplished musician, composer, singer, instruments player and sound engineer. He has more than a dozen albums to his credit so far. (SoulMelodies.com) His varied interests include alternative holistic living, Vedic studies, social criticism, environment, linguistics, history, art & crafts, nature studies, web technologies etc.

Many of his books have been acclaimed internationally and translated in other languages.

By The Same Author

Oil-Final Countdown To A Global Crisis And Its Solutions

End of Modern Civilization And Alternative Future

To Kill Cow Means To End Human Civilization

Cow And Humanity - Made For Each Other

Cows Are Cool - Love 'Em!

Let's Be Friends - A Curious, Calm Cow

Wondrous Glories of Vraja

We Feel Just Like You Do

Tsunami Of Diseases Headed Our Way - Know Your Food Before Time Runs Out

Cow Killing And Beef Export - The Master Plan To Turn India Into A Desert
By 2050

Capitalism Communism And Cowism - A New Economics For The 21st Century

Noble Cow - Munching Grass, Looking Curious And Just Hanging Around

Spare Us Some Carcasses - An Appeal From The Vultures

To Save Time Is To Lengthen Life

Life Is Nothing But Time - Time Is Life, Life Is Time

An Inch of Time Can Not Be Bought With A Mile of Gold

Lost Time Is Never Found Again

Cow Dung - A Down-To- Earth Solution To Global Warming And Climate
Change

Cow Dung For Food Security And Survival of Human Race

(More information on availability on DrDasa.com)

www.ingramcontent.com/pod-product-compliance
Lightning Source LLC
Chambersburg PA
CBHW070646030426
42337CB00020B/4182